PRIVATE ENTERPRISE AND SOCIALISM in the MIDDLE EAST

Howard S. Ellis

AMERICAN ENTERPRISE INSTITUTE
FOR PUBLIC POLICY RESEARCH
1200 17th Street, N.W.
Washington, D.C. 20036
October 1970

AMERICAN ENTERPRISE INSTITUTE
for Public Policy Research

Middle East Research Project

Professor George Lenczowski
University of California, Berkeley
Director

91st Congress
Second Session

ANALYSIS NO. 17

This Special Analysis is presented by the American Enterprise Institute as the fourth in its series within the framework of the Middle East Research Project.

Howard S. Ellis, Flood Professor of Economics (Emeritus) at the University of California, Berkeley, is an expert in the economic problems of developing countries.

The author bespeaks his sincere thanks and his obligations to Professor George Lenczowski for the inspiration and insights which accrue from his profound knowledge of the Middle East; to Professor Bent Hansen for materials and a critical reading of the chapter on Egypt; and to Professor Memduh Yasa for valuable suggestions concerning the economy of Turkey.

CONTENTS

INTRODUCTION

The Middle East today is caught up in rapid and almost convulsive changes. To understand the nature of these changes, one needs to proceed in an order which reverses the Marxian materialistic interpretation of history. According to that doctrine, the "mode of production" determines the nature of the economy, of the culture, of politics, and even of religion. In the Middle East, the cradle and chief point of mutual impact of three great world religions—Muslim, Christian, and Jewish—the reverse is more nearly the case. The foreign and domestic politics of the countries of the region largely respond to religious-cultural differences, and economic policy in the main follows as a consequence.

Political Change in the Middle East

As in other parts of the world, the first world war set afoot a process of change which has gone on in the Middle East with a tempo of spasmodic but—if possible—increasing intensity ever since. At the beginning of the nineteenth century, Persia and Turkey controlled the region; but European colonization, spheres of influence, and mandates after the first world war fractured this dual control. By 1939, there were eight nominally sovereign nations, though generally under European tutelage; by now, eighteen nations occupy the same territory, most of them independent, and only tiny areas are under foreign sovereignty.[1] Even more important is the transformation of the political character of the new regimes.

Legislative bodies, originally established to advise foreign rulers in Egypt, Syria, and Iraq have come to be mere appendages to totalitarian regimes. With the probable exceptions of Lebanon and Israel, the military—sometimes held in check by a strong executive—is in the saddle; or a king, sheik, or premier rules single-handedly. Purely personal freedom varies greatly from one country to another. But constitutionalism and political and economic liberalism, having flourished for a while in the twenties and early thirties, suffered from the Great Depression, the second world war and its attending interruption of foreign armies and inflations, and finally collapsed in all but a few countries under the rivalry of the USSR and the West, the rise of Nasser in Egypt, and the ground swell of resentment against Israel. While some variant of

---

[1] J. H. Thompson and R. D. Reischauer, eds., *Modernization of the Arab World* (Princeton, N.J.: D. van Nostrand Co., Inc., 1966), p. 2.

socialism is widespread in the Middle East, democracy in any recognizable form has largely disappeared because it lacked foundations in a thriving middle class and a tradition of self-government.

Nationalism and socialism are kindred systems in general, just as internationalism and private enterprise (or "capitalism") are akin. But in the Middle East, nationalism and socialism are especially closely related. Both are in some measure reactions from the earlier foreign, that is to say, European, political and economic domination. The conjoined reaction does not always appear, as for example in Lebanon and Iran, but it is a common phenomenon in both Arab and non-Arab countries. In the Arab countries, the resentment of a foreign presence in political and economic matters has taken on a particularly virulent anti-Western form because of a combination of xenophobia with a sense of outrage over the existence of a Jewish state in the midst of the Arab world. The United States is the special repository for these hostile sentiments, not because of mandates or extensive business interests in prewar days, as was the case with France or England, but because it is rich and powerful, the chief protagonist of the West, and friendly to Israel. "No observer of present trends in the Arab world can fail to be impressed by the strength of its revulsion against Western political and economic values and ideologies," writes Professor Issawi.[2] Authoritarian rule settled down upon the Arabs, says Professor Morroe Berger; "Social equality rather than political freedom was emphasized. National Power rather than individual freedom was held out as the primary aim."[3] This is true also for most of the non-Arab Middle East.

A word is in order concerning the role of the military in the recent history of this region. In Europe and in Latin America, the army has generally represented conservative or even reactionary political positions. But in the Middle East, this generalization does not always hold. Before these nations attained their independence, young army officers or prospective officers were amongst the most numerous visitors, often for protracted sojourns, in Western countries. In the absence of a substantial middle class or influential number of intellectuals, they became in many cases the chief bearers of advanced ideas of progress and the agents of reform or revolutionary change. Having come into power, they have, in a number of cases, allowed the civil service to be filled by capable persons outside the army. Thus there arose a combination of great rarity in the West: an authoritarian reform or socialist government backed by the military. Unfortunately, as in the most recent annals of Iraq, military rule cannot be counted upon for devotion to the general welfare. But it is important to bear in mind, as General Glubb points out, that the detestation of military rule per se, which is part of Anglo-Saxon morals, is quite foreign to Arab traditions.[4]

Unfortunately for economic development, which requires above everything else domestic peace and tranquillity, the authoritarianism of the Middle East has never been able to devise an accepted rule for succession in political power. This was true even in the politico-religious sphere of succession to the Prophet: no established rule existed for selection of the caliphs. In the more purely political field, neither was there an acceptance of hereditary monarchical succession nor of parliamentary or popular election. The result of this vacuum in a critical area is authoritarian regimes

[2] *Ibid.*, p. 13.
[3] Morroe Berger, *The Arab World Today* (Garden City, N.Y.: Doubleday and Co., 1964), p. 306.
[4] Thompson and Reischauer, *op. cit.*, p. 60.

without stability, the worse parts of two systems. The working of the combination is intensified by the nature of the peasants, who tend to be bound by tradition and to be politically acquiescent, and by the paucity and character of the middle class. In Egypt this class has been estimated at no more than 6 percent of the population;[5] and, as a stabilizing factor, its composition currently is reduced by the substitution of civil servants for independent employers.

It would, of course, be wrong to convey the impression that all political or cultural change in the Middle East has negative value. The improved status of women is undeniable, particularly in Egypt and Turkey. Aside from its own intrinsic value, it may contribute in the long run to an improvement of government. So too may the increase of literacy and the betterment of public health. Furthermore, there is probably a slow drift toward more equalitarian distribution of wealth and income, a statistically elusive matter. It is difficult, however, to detect among all the good and bad changes any pronounced tendency toward more stable governments, which could provide continuity in economic policies and economic growth. In Egypt, internal strife was diverted toward external crises, with no improvement from an economic angle.

Peculiarities of Economic Development in the Middle East

The most dramatic distinguishing characteristic of economic development in the Middle East is the fact that its rate of growth, at least so far as concerns the gross domestic product (GDP), has been the highest in the world during the decades of the fifties and sixties. This seems to be a safe generalization, despite the pitfalls of statistics of the region and the difficulty of the very definition of the region itself. These difficulties are not reduced by the pervasive political turmoil in this part of the world, which accounts for the absence of any United Nations regional economic office, because of Arab objections to Israeli membership in that organization. But for the Middle East, defined very narrowly as Iran, Iraq, Israel, Jordan, Lebanon, Syria, and Egypt, the annual increase of GDP for the period 1950–67 at 6.5 percent exceeds the next category, Southern Europe, at 6.0 percent, and all countries classified by the World Bank as "developing," at 5 percent.[6] This position would not be substantially changed by the inclusion of Turkey and Egypt, which are included in most definitions of the Middle East.

Reinforcing the highly aggregative economic magnitude of gross domestic product is the behavior of a number of more specific categories. When "developing countries" are divided into the following groups—Africa, South Asia, East Asia, Southern Europe, Latin America, and the Middle East—it is the last of these which shows the *highest rate* of annual increase in *all* of the following respects: GNP, 7.2 percent (1960–67); agricultural production, 4.1 percent (1960–66); industrial production, 10.8 percent (1960–67); electric energy output, 18.3 percent (1948–67); steel consumption, 11.3 percent (1950/52–67); enrollment in primary schools, 8.5 percent, in secondary schools, 13.4 percent (1950–65).[7]

---

[5] Berger, *op. cit.*, pp. 252–53.

[6] Commission on International Development, *Partners in Development* (New York: Praeger Publishers, 1969), Table 1, pp. 358–59.

[7] *Ibid.*, pp. 28, 31, 32, 36, 39, 40, and 42.

Enthusiasm for these extraordinarily high rates of increase should be tempered, perhaps, by two other considerations: first, in most cases, these are increases from very low initial values; second, genuine economic development does not necessarily result from such increases, however important each may be. Still, the general showing of the Middle East is impressive.

The second distinctive feature of the economic development of the region is the prominent role played by oil production. This is so much a matter of common knowledge that the high rates of development which have been achieved by countries such as Turkey and Lebanon, which have no oil, or by Egypt, which has very little, are apt to be forgotten. Nevertheless, the natural resources of the region other than petroleum are not noteworthy. The Nile, Litani, and the Tigris and Euphrates rivers are, of course, productive. But more than half of the area of the whole region is desert, and in some countries less than half the land is cultivated. Where agriculture relies upon rainfall, it is often highly seasonal, and sometimes unreliable and scarce. Mineral wealth aside from oil is limited to a few regions.

Who can fail to be impressed, however, with the endowment of the 135 million inhabitants of the Middle East—roughly 3.6 percent of the world's population— with 36 percent of the free world's petroleum production, and an estimated 68 percent of the free world's petroleum reserves?[8] While the United States accounts for 29 percent of world production, it possesses only 8 percent of total reserves; and these and the Middle East portions leave for "others" 35 and 24 percent respectively of production and reserves. Oil royalties for Middle Eastern countries have mounted from $1,068,000,000 in 1957 to $2,888,000,000 in 1967;[9] they provide as much as 90 percent of total government revenues in Saudi Arabia, Kuwait, Qatar, and Abu Dhabi.

But oil has not been an unmixed blessing. According to the testimony of Brigadier-General Longrigg, a British expert on the oil industry, "all this wealth . . . represents money-bags from a single source, handed free of charge or effort to the national government, to be diffused by it *tant bien que mal* to the population . . . . It also does little to enhance a true popular comprehension of economic facts." Much of the expenditure is of dubious effectiveness "by reason of the imperfection of economic and political vision, the scarcity of really competent planners, some reluctance to act on expert advice (especially if offered by foreigners), and a tendency to hastiness and inadequate study of projects."[10] Despite all of this, it would be folly to believe that the Middle East has not derived immense economic gains from oil. What the future may hold is another matter, later to be considered.

Another peculiarity of Middle Eastern economic development is what one writer on Egypt has called the "heavy-industry syndrome." In that country it resulted in the doubtfully rational Helwan iron and steel works; in Turkey in the Karabük complex, also economically questionable in several aspects; even Israel must have its steel plant. The doubts do not pertain to industry in general, but to heavy industry; but they remain as doubts even in countries like Egypt and Iraq, which have invested heavily in agriculture. At the opposite extreme is a tendency toward extravagance in "showcase" projects. Thus Egypt's Voice of the Arabs broadcasting station is said to

---

[8] U.S. AID, *Economic Data Book, Near East and South Asia*, NESA Regional, September 1969, p. 5.
[9] *The New Middle East*, September 1969, p. 32.
[10] Thompson and Reischauer, *op. cit.*, p. 111.

involve a budgetary load as heavy as the United States' Voice of America! Some of these cases of ostentatious consumption expenditure apparently illustrate the "easy come, easy go" of oil revenues, such as Saudi Arabia's $3 million radio transmitters, or Algeria's $20 million international fairgrounds and $30 million convention hall.

Extravagant outlays of this sort and the high rates of increase in economic magnitudes previously alluded to should not conceal the modest level of economic life in the Middle East for most of its inhabitants. Excluding such nontypical cases as Kuwait, Israel, and Lebanon, per capita gross national product generally ranges between $168 for Egypt and Iran's $304. This is better than East Asia's $140 (excluding Japan), or Africa's $130 (excluding South Africa), but falls considerably short of the $410 of South America, and far below the $2,480 of Western Europe, North America, Australia, and New Zealand. Even these figures probably do not reveal the poverty of the populace generally as clearly as more specific magnitudes. For purposes of comparing with the "total Near East" figures the United States data are given in parenthesis: life expectancy, 50 years (70); infant mortality per 1,000, 114.9 (23); inhabitants per hospital bed, 482 (113); inhabitants per physician, 2,273 (674); students as percent of 5–19 age group, 39 (84); literacy rate, percent 36 (98).[11]

Finally it cannot be too much emphasized that the growth figures cited in earlier pages pertain to national *totals*. When divided out over the population, they often shrink to appallingly low amounts. Thus it can be said with full justification that "the most serious dilemma of economic development is posed by rapid population growth."[12]

The United States and the USSR in the Middle East

Aside from the struggle between Nasserism and separate national loyalties, and the pitting of Arabism against Israel, the most lively opposition of interests in the Middle East is the rivalry of the United States and the USSR. Since the latter country seems currently in the ascendancy, an economic analysis looking to the future must be concerned with this conflict.

After the first world war, the United States refused to accept a mandate over Armenia but was drawn into Middle Eastern affairs by the Zionist question, the exigencies of oil supply, and the requirements of defense.[13] In the thirties, Communist parties began to be formed in Egypt, Syria, and Iraq, but during this decade the USSR did not push its interests aggressively. However, in the forties the increasing activities of that country caused Turkey and Greece to feel menaced, and their situation impelled President Truman, in his message to Congress in March 1947, to request authority to furnish military and economic aid to those countries and the "northern tier" of Arab countries.

The United States entered into a military assistance pact with Iraq in April 1954, and with Pakistan in May of the same year. In February 1955, Iraq signed an agreement with Turkey, later joined by Iran and other countries, in what came to be called

---

[11] U.S. AID, *Economic Data Book, Near East and South Asia.* The figures generally pertain to 1967 and 1968.

[12] Thompson and Reischauer, *op. cit.*, p. 62.

[13] Royal Institute of International Affairs, Sir Reader Bullard, ed., *The Middle East*, 3d ed. (London: Oxford University Press, 1958). This source is drawn upon extensively for the following account; cf. pp. 4–42.

5

the Baghdad Pact. Through Turkey, the signatories were linked to NATO and through Pakistan to SEATO. The Baghdad Pact infuriated Nasser and angered the Soviet Union. In October 1955, Nasser concluded a military alliance with Syria and Saudi Arabia, joined by Jordan a year later. Nasser proclaimed himself the liberator of the Arab world and the champion of Africa. The Arabs began talking of the elimination of Israel. In 1956 and 1957 Nasser seemed to have attained virtual hegemony over much of the Arab Middle East.

In his January 1957 message to Congress, President Eisenhower emphasized the importance of the Middle East to the United States and asked for authority to aid in the economic development of the region and to use United States military forces if necessary to protect the territorial integrity of Middle Eastern nations. The "Eisenhower Doctrine" tended, contrary to its intention, of course, to increase the popularity of the USSR in certain countries which already highly regarded it as a country of exemplary progress and economic development, with no territorial possessions, oil concessions, or bases in the Middle East. Moreover, the Soviet authoritarian regime was more easily understood in parts of the region than the ideals and character of the democratic governments of the West.

A high point of cooperation between international communism and Arabism was reached late in 1957 with the convening of an Afro-Asian Peoples' Conference in Cairo. During the next year, however, the revolution in Iraq and underground Communist activity in Syria dissuaded Nasser from too great involvement with the USSR. After the United States declined to participate in the building of the Aswan Dam, Nasser turned with alacrity to the USSR in 1958 and secured its help in completing this project; it has substantial economic value and great symbolic significance in the Arab world for Egypt's prestige and leadership. In the ensuing decade, most countries of the Middle East have kept on good terms with the Soviet Union, but have stopped short of being pulled into it.

In addition to emergency relief given to various Middle Eastern countries in the immediate postwar period, the United States concluded agreements with most of them and extended substantial financial and technical assistance beginning in the early fifties.[14] Soviet assistance, though in general smaller, has shown a gradual increase in the area while American aid has been declining. This situation will be reviewed in the final chapter with some observations on desirable policy.

It is the purpose of the present study to present a summary view and analysis of recent economic developments in the Middle East. To avoid running to encyclopaedic length, the method chosen is to deal with a few important and representative countries. While Israel would have presented many illuminating features, it is not included because it is in most respects not typical of the Middle East. As representatives of non-Arab countries and important in their own right, Turkey and Iran represent the "northern tier." Egypt clearly is the leader of the Arab group, belongs to the south, and is interesting for the economist. Egypt and Iraq are socialist in some degree or other; but Lebanon affords an example of the workings of private enterprise, and Turkey and Iran rely upon it extensively. Among these five countries Iraq and Iran, in contrast with the others, possess large petroleum resources. The analysis begins with Egypt in recognition that, despite Nasser's failure to achieve a united Arab republic, his country occupies a prestigious position in the Middle East.

---

[14] The figures for United States aid in the Middle East appear in the Appendix, p. 119.

6

I. EGYPT: "ARAB SOCIALISM"

The Character of "Arab Socialism"

"Arab socialism" and Egypt are one. Perhaps the course of future events will alter this dictum, but at the present, with the withdrawal of Syria from the United Arab Republic after a few years' membership in the union, Egyptian economic arrangements really constitute "Arab socialism." Other Arab countries (Iraq and Syria) have also come definitively into the socialist fold, but even so, Egypt—by reason of its size and leadership in the Arab world—will probably remain the exemplar of this kind of socialism. Needless to say, it differs from the socialism of Norway as greatly as from that of the USSR.

Like any truly socialist country, the government of Egypt has come to own the chief industrial means of production. It does not own the cultivated land or conduct the farming, though the weighty agricultural cooperatives are supervised by the government, nor does it engage to any large extent in retail trade or operate the small producer units. Though government influences wages through minimum wage laws and its dominant position as an employer, it leaves personal incomes in considerable degree to the market forces of supply and demand.

Another conspicuous characteristic of Egyptian socialism is its intense nationalism, or even chauvinism. One of the leading Egyptologists in economic affairs, Professor Charles Issawi, refers to "the long period of foreign domination, stretching unbroken from the Persian conquest in 525 B.C. to the 19th century," and observes that "several millenia of centralized autocracy have accustomed Egypt to look to the government to initiate any business whatsoever."[1] These facts help to account at once for both the socialism and the xenophobia which have prevailed under the caption of "Egyptianization."

Aside from the nationalism which strongly imbued the revolution of 1952, there was an initial absence of ideologies, Marxian or otherwise, despite the fact that it was precipitated by a sharp economic downturn. In the course of time, however, the pronouncements of President Gamal Abdel Nasser have taken on a more and more Marxian color; but it is difficult to know how deep-seated is this philosophy in either

---

[1] Charles Issawi, *Egypt in Revolution: an Economic Analysis* (London: Oxford University Press, 1963), pp. 5, 7.

his own thinking or that of the regime generally. The regime, however, is clearly socialist.

A fourth fairly clear differentiating feature of Arab socialism as defined by Egyptian practice is its emphasis upon capital formation as the chief economic control apparatus, on the side of both the supply of capital in domestic saving and foreign borrowing, and of the demand for investment purposes.

It would be very natural, indeed, on the basis of the enumerated four cardinal features of Arab socialism for anyone to object: "But these are exactly the characteristics which have been set forth for the Turkish economic system! Just how, then, does Arab *socialism* differ, if at all, from the Turkish state *capitalism*?" The answer surely must be that the resemblances are genuine, but that there are important differences which justify the contrasting designations.

In the first place, while the Egyptian army officers and their spokesmen in the revolution hastened to reassure the owners of capital that there was no thought of abandoning private enterprise, no such sentiments have been heard during the present decade. Turkey, on the contrary, continues to profess loyalty to a market-oriented private enterprise system.

Secondly, the Ataturk revolution was in large part directed toward a supposed foreign economic domination of the country, whereas the Egyptian revolution, which quickly became Nasser's revolution, was, indeed, xenophobic, but directed more strongly against the wealthy citizens at home, particularly landowners, who controlled the country politically. This was evidenced by the speed with which land reform measures were introduced, not principally for any supposed virtues of productivity, but on equalitarian, political, and economic grounds.

Thirdly, and possibly related to the second point, there is a good deal of open unemployment in Turkey, whereas in Egypt part of the unemployment is concealed in the services, including quite conspicuously the government.

The fourth and fifth points are political rather than economic, but their economic implications are numerous. The state capitalism of Turkey is not unrelated to the orientation of the country toward the West, whereas Egypt departs more and more from its international ambivalence, becoming more and more involved with the USSR. Parallel to this development Egypt seems virtually a totalitarian and dictatorial government while Turkey, despite the hovering of the military in the wings, continues to maintain a parliamentary system with competing political parties. But one observer points out that Egypt's ruler does not have a party organization which permeates into all levels of economic and political activity; this renders the execution of government plans more difficult but makes life easier for the common man than in other totalitarian states.

The Evolution of Arab Socialism

Egypt Before the Socialist Revolution

Historians generally regard Muhammad Ali as the creator of modern Egypt. A native of Albania, he took part in the expulsion by the British and Turks in 1801 of the French regime, which survived from the Napoleonic invasion. In 1805 he became the Viceroy of Egypt and soon began a vigorous program of industrialization in order to establish economic independence for the country. He introduced railroads, launched irrigation works, and created a number of state industries. Government controls permeated all phases of economic activity and are said to have exceeded those of the contemporary Egyptian socialism because they included minute prescription of agricultural processes. In the century following his death in 1849, paternalism of this sort generally receded, save for brief revivals of his ideas under Khedive Ismail (1863–79) and Ismail Sidky Pasha following 1920.

Economic development in Egypt during the first half of the present century was slow; in 1950, with a per capita income of $118, the country remained in a low bracket among underdeveloped regions. Life expectancy at birth for males was 36, compared to the U.S. figure of 69. From 1913 to 1928, gross domestic product (GDP) had increased only at 1 percent per annum, from 1928 to 1939 at $1\frac{1}{2}$ percent, and from 1939 to 1950 at $2\frac{1}{2}$, only to fall back to virtual stagnation from 1950–55. But even when GDP increased, the population explosion which followed the introduction of antibiotics slowed down the growth of per capita income to a barely visible one-tenth of 1 percent per annum. Despite these attributes of economic underdevelopment, Egypt was not in all respects a typical representative of this condition. Her transport and communication systems were adequate, the techniques of irrigation and drainage were sophisticated, the organization of the cotton trade highly developed, and by 1954, 55 percent of enterprises had assumed the corporate form.[2]

At mid-century, agriculture provided one-third of the national product and two-thirds of the employment, and exports of raw cotton fetched 80 percent of the foreign exchange income. Every available acre of land in the Nile Valley was utilized for cotton, cereals, and, less frequently, for vegetables and fruits. For some crops, per acre yields were the highest in the world, but the pressure of population tended to create overt rural unemployment and a crowding of people into the cities. With improved agricultural techniques, part of the labor force could have been released, some say as much as one-third. High rents on land and low wages allowed the peasants slight chance of rising above bare subsistence income or of escaping from the gamut of crippling or debilitating diseases.

During the thirties, Egyptian industry began to expand because, having secured tariff autonomy at the beginning of the decade, the government had raised protective tariffs on imported consumer goods; the Great Depression deflected capital investment into agriculture, while the Bank Misr provided working capital and advice. Egyptian industry expanded during the decade of the thirties through import substitution. This was followed by the second world war with a strong stimulus to industry through the magnitude of British military expenditures. Egyptian industry continued to operate in a seller's market for five years after the war, building and refurbishing its equipment.

However, by the end of the decade of the forties, the process of import substitution was beginning to play out for two reasons: limits were being set on the domestic market by the stagnant income level in agriculture; and foreign outlets for textiles and food were not expanding. Manufacturing was concentrated in a small number of

[2] The description of the Egyptian economy before and following the revolution of 1952 given in the preceding paragraph and the following pages is based largely upon Patrick O'Brien, *The Revolution in Egypt's Economic System: from Private Enterprise to Socialism 1952–1965*, Royal Institute of International Affairs (London: Oxford University Press, 1966).

9

large firms producing sugar, cotton yarn, rayon, cement, and chemical fertilizers, but the strength of these concerns rested on monopoly, rather than efficiency. It is said that the greatest obstacle to improving the competitiveness of Egyptian industry was the poor quality and high prices of domestic raw materials. Though wages lagged, this did not redound greatly to the benefit of profits because labor productivity was low, the result of inadequate diets and lack of vocational education. On the eve of the revolution, the economy was stagnant. The years 1950–52 were characterized by the Federation of Egyptian Industry as a period of excess capacity, unemployment, falling profits, and crisis. But this was partly due to the collapse of the Korean war boom.

Historical Phases of Development under the Revolutionary Government

The Free Enterprise Stage, 1952–56

"When the Free Officers seized power in July, 1952, they were without an economic ideology," writes Patrick O'Brien, and the tentative steps taken—though generally all in one direction—for nearly a decade until the wave of nationalizations in 1961–63 bear out this statement. Yet the economic background sketched in the preceding paragraphs supplies part of the explanation of a revolutionary movement, despite the protestation of its officials that Egypt could prosper only under free enterprise.

Furthermore, one of the first incisive steps of the new government was an economic measure—the famous Land Reform Act of September 8, 1952. It affected only 10 percent of the land area, providing for a maximum limit on land ownership of 200 acres (later substantially lowered). Land in excess of this amount was to be requisitioned by the government over a period of five years, paid for in 3 percent bonds, the requisitioned land to be distributed to small landlords and farm laborers in 2–5 acre plots per family. They were to pay for the land over 30 years with interest at 3 percent, during which period the land could not be sold. This measure will be the subject of further analysis, but it is worth noting now that its primary aim was the redistribution of income, not agricultural development; it produced a shock out of all proportion to its economic magnitude because it was revolutionary in its political effects, being aimed initially at the royal family and 15 to 20 wealthy families.[3]

By July 1953, the government had produced a Three Year Plan which followed earlier plans for public investment along conventional lines,[4] but was unconventional in actually being put into effect! The state participated in the founding of the Helwan iron and steel plant near Cairo, contributing half of its capital, the balance subscribed by private firms. Also the Free Officers were responsible for launching the ambitious Aswan High Dam project, though work was only begun four years later when water rights had been settled with the Sudan and when financing had been obtained from the USSR.

Aside from these major investment projects in this period, the Revolutionary government promulgated a new company law compelling directors to retire at 60, setting a maximum to their remuneration, and limiting the number of directorships held by

---

[3] The *locus classicus* for analysis of this measure is Doreen Warriner's *Land Reform and Development in the Middle East*, 1st ed., 1957, 2d ed., 1962 (London: Oxford University Press), pp. 14 and 15 in the 2d edition.

[4] Such as the first and second Five Year Plans, launched in 1935 and 1945.

10

one person. It is said that the new regime did everything conceivable to give incentive and protection to private concerns, and that it usually consulted the Federation of Egyptian Industries on economic measures. It amended the existing legislation in order to permit agricultural laborers to organize; strikes were made illegal, labor disputes being settled by compulsory arbitration.

However, during the 1952–57 quinquennium events and forces were moving the government away from its initial positions. A potent influence turning Nasser from the West was the Soviet ambassador to Egypt in 1953, David Solod. Because of the wild fluctuations of price in the Alexandria market, sales of cotton to the United Kingdom fell off, prompting Egypt to seek outlets in the Soviet satellites. In August 1955, Nasser announced the conclusion of an arrangement with Czechoslovakia for the delivery of large quantities of military equipment, including Soviet aircraft, in exchange for cotton, an announcement which was received with tremendous enthusiasm throughout the Arab world. Then came the withdrawal of the American offer of finance for the Aswan Dam, the Suez Canal controversy ending in the nationalization of the canal on July 26, 1956. This was the beginning of systematic elimination of foreign businesses (the "Egyptianizing" process), and finally the humiliating defeat of Egypt in the war with Israel. These events marked the end of Egyptian tolerance of free enterprise, of foreigners, and of amicable relations with Western Europe and America.

The Controlled Capitalist Economy, 1956–60

By a presidential decree of 1957 a National Planning Committee was established as a technical secretariat composed of 200 government officials. But the next industrial Five Year Plan, put into operation in 1958 and aiming at a 6 percent annual increase of industrial output, resembled its predecessors in that, in O'Brien's phrase, "it merely catalogued a lengthy and often contradictory list of priorities" without much attention to their financing and execution.

Apparently during these years, private business was supposed to furnish the driving force of economic activity, while the extent of government control could be indefinitely extended. Thus in 1957 all public industrial and commercial property was put under the aegis of an "Economic Organization," which controlled nearly one-third of the output of the economy and employed one-fifth of the labor force. If the state owned 25 percent of the shares of a company, the Economic Organization could appoint a majority of the directors and the managing director. In 1959, the Ministry of Industry was empowered to regulate the establishment, expansion, purpose, and location of all plants. Finally, in 1959 corporate dividends were put under state regulation, an amount equal to 5 percent being set aside for the purchase of government bonds.

In addition to these measures, the Bank Misr established undertakings in shipping, publishing, insurance, and hotels, while the Misr Group, a designation introduced February 13, 1960, produced chemicals, pharmaceuticals, edible oils, cement, and textiles, which it dominated with 60 percent of the output. By 1959 the Group was responsible for half of the production by "private enterprise" under the Plan. Furthermore, in the sphere of finance the Economic Organization controlled seven commercial banks with half the outstanding loans in the country and five insurance companies which accounted for 68 percent of the total business in that field. In January 1957 all foreign-owned banks, insurance companies, and commercial agenices were obliged to convert into domestic-owned joint stock companies within five years. By the end of the decade, controls vastly outweighed capitalism on the Egyptian scene. Whereas in 1952–53 approximately three-fourths of gross capital formation was private, in 1959–60 this same proportion was in the hands of the state.

The First Five Year Plan, 1960–65

While the five-year period 1960–65 witnessed the virtual extinction of private enterprise in Egypt, this does not seem to have been the animus of the Plan as formulated at the beginning of the period. The rationale of policy was, initially as it had been in the past, that the state should exercise economic domination by controlling investment, while the private sector supplied the capital. Some four-fifths of all investment contemplated for the biennium 1960–62 was to be public, and this predominance of the government antedated the nationalizations of 1961 and 1963. To the private sector there remained 60 percent of building construction, investments in trade and commerce, and 25 percent of investment in industry.

On the side of the supply of capital, on the other hand, during the first biennium of the Plan, 20 percent was supposed to flow in from abroad and 70 percent from domestic private sources, leaving a modest 10 percent to the public saving. The government prescribed maximum dividend rates for corporations, set at 10 percent in 1958, but under protest the rates were raised to 20 percent later. Since this measure could scarcely be expected to encourage private saving, the government attempted to do so by a series of *ad hoc* devices, in part involving special fiscal measures, and in part resting on favorable interest rates on various types of saving. It is a matter of record that these special incentives were not notably successful. The failure to evoke adequate flows of private savings was undoubtedly a major factor in unleashing the nationalizations (not contemplated in the Plan) of 1961 and 1963.

These cataclysms were preceded by minor tremors: in June 1960, the newspapers were taken over by the Misr Group, and they were followed by the tea trade and pharmaceuticals. In June 1961, the Alexandria futures market was closed, and the Egyptian Cotton Commission took over the buying and selling of raw cotton at fixed prices. In July 1961, the Khedival Shipping Line was nationalized, and in the same month not only were the banks taken over completely, but also 44 concerns in the timber industry, in cement, copper, and electricity. Compensation for private owners was relatively small. In May 1962, President Nasser gave to the Congress the famous "Charter," assigning to the public sector investment in the infrastructure, heavy and medium industry, and trade and financial operations; and to the private sector, land, buildings, construction, light industry, and internal trade. By the end of 1963, almost all large companies in all fields had been nationalized, embracing 40 percent of GNP.

Professor Hansen believes that at first the nationalizations "just happened"; but subsequently an ideology was evolved to justify them: (1) protecting the working population from exploitation, and (2) mobilizing national savings. It would be more appropriate, he observes, to recast these reasons as follows: (1) diversion of profits from lavish consumer expenditures to investment for development, and (2) the reallocation of national savings.[5] The results of the First Five Year Plan follow:

[5] Bent Hansen and Girgis A. Marzouk, *Development and Economic Policy in the U.A.R., Egypt* (Amsterdam, Holland: North-Holland Publishing Co., 1965), pp. 168–69.

12

National Income from Main Sectors (E£ million)

Industry	1959–60	1964–65
Agriculture	405.0	477.0
Industry	256.3	385.0
Electricity	9.8	22.4
Transport and communications	92.9	157.6
Housing construction	73.0	80.1
Services	265.5	387.9
Others, not specified	182.5	252.2
Total national income	1,285.0	1,762.2

Source: Donald C. Mead, *Growth and Structural Change in the Egyptian Economy* (Homewood, Illinois: Richard D. Irwin, Inc., 1967), p. 53, fn. 18.

Economic Survey by Sectors

Agriculture

It is traditional but still appropriate to begin a description of Egypt's agriculture with the dictum of Herodotus that "Egypt is the gift of the Nile." The annual burden of fertile silt borne down to the fields of the valley is the factor which primarily enables 97 percent of the country's population of 32 million to live on 3 percent of its area, a density of five per cultivated acre, one of the highest in the world. But Herodotus' statement, while pertinent to most of Egypt's five millenia of history, needs to be qualified today in two respects. In the first place, the fertility of the valley is not altogether a gift of nature: the substitution of perennial irrigation for the old basin system has multiplied annual yields by threefold. In the second place, since 1945 agriculture has fallen from 40 to only 25 percent of national income. However, this unduly minimizes its importance, since agriculture provides one-half of total employment; since much of commerce and finance turns upon cotton and other crops; and, finally, since industry depends on domestic agricultural materials.

Furthermore, while the share of agriculture has fallen markedly, its output in absolute amount has risen by more than half since 1946. Both the absolute increase and

Index of Agricultural Output in Egypt (1935–39 = 100)

Year	Index	Year	Index	Year	Index
1946	98	1954	126	1962	151
1947	100	1955	128	1963	152
1948	113	1956	133	1964	158
1949	114	1957	144	1965	161
1950	114	1958	143	1966	161
1951	110	1959	149	1967	156
1952	119	1960	153		
1953	114	1961	135		

Source: U.N. Food and Agriculture Organization, *Production* volumes; figures 1960–67 given on 1952–56 base adjusted to continue on 1935–39 base.

13

the failure of this increase to keep up with the advance of other sectors are important facts in Egyptian economic life. The former has come about in part through the greater application of human labor, but at diminishing returns, to which we shall return under the second head. More important have been the increases of "area cultivated" and "area cropped." If a plot of land produces not one but three crops per annum, the second magnitude rises by threefold. From a base in 1897 (=100), area cultivated rose in 1960 to 118, while area cropped rose to 155. Thus the pressing down of the intensive margin of cultivation has meant more for output than extending the extensive margin.

Aside from increased area and cropping and the use of insecticides and pesticides, Professor Hansen ascribes great significance to the decreased application of artificial fertilizers. Thus, over the years 1937–47 "the 25 percent fall in fertilizers, plus delayed effects from the much lower supply of fertilizers and the unhappy crop rotation during the war, was sufficient to wipe out the effects on total production of a simultaneous increase in land by 8 percent, animals by 22 percent, canals and dams by 17 percent and pumps by 14 percent." This, he believes, reveals that "we are very far away indeed from the Malthusian nightmares usually associated with the agricultural situation in underdeveloped countries."[6]

However that may be, the growth of population denied to the individual agricultural laborer the fruits of increased total agricultural product. The result was that, despite the substantial increase in total output, productivity per person did not grow in 1960 over the level prevailing before the first world war, and wages conformed closely to productivity. Improvement in agricultural techniques, extensions of land cultivated, and heavier cropping did not solve the problem of rural poverty.

Number of Persons Occupied in Agriculture
(in millions)

1907	2.40	1937	4.28
1917	2.82	1947	4.22
1927	3.50	1960	4.40

Source: *Annuaire Statistique.*

Does this statement also include the famous Land Reform Act of 1952? Such was the character of the measure and its subsequent complements that—despite amelioration of the lot of the peasants in certain ways—the answer must nevertheless be affirmative. To make an appreciable effect on poverty, an agricultural measure would have to concern itself primarily with productivity; but, as we have already observed, this was not the case in Egypt. On the authority of Doreen Warriner, an outstanding specialist on this subject, the purposes were three: to expropriate holdings of very wealthy landowners in excess of 300 acres and redistribute them,[7] to lower rents to a maximum of seven times the basic land tax, and to raise agricultural wages by stipulating a minimum rate. All three of these purposes were concerned with the distribution of wealth and income, not with productivity. If the poverty-level incomes of the peasants

[6] Hansen and Marzouk, *op. cit.*, p. 77.
[7] The act of 1952 set the maximum at 200 acres, but this was raised in 1958 to 300. This figure was in turn reduced, as described below.

were to be raised merely by redistributive measures, they would have had to be much more severe than they ever were or ever became. Only one-tenth of the land area was originally liable to redistribution; the maximum holding of 300 acres permitted a yearly rent income of E£ 5,000–E£ 6,000 ($8,400 to $11,200 at the exchange rate then prevailing), a really handsome income in a poor country; and finally the minimum wage proved unenforceable.

On July 15, 1961, a second Land Reform Act was put into effect by presidential decree. It lowered the limit of land holding to 100 acres; exempted one-half of the price of distributed land from what the purchaser had to pay, and abolished interest on balances owing; and introduced a progressive tax on rents of residential property. In 1969 the maximum limit on land ownership was lowered to 25 acres.

The results of the land reform in both the narrower sense of redistribution of land and the broader sense of a complex of measures bettering the peasants' general situation may be summarized under four captions:

1. Landowning is less unequal: the number of owners in the 1–5 feddan group (1 feddan equals 1.038 acres) increased from 22.5 to 30.8 percent of the total area while the over-200 group fell from 19.8 to 6.8 percent.[8] Furthermore, the well-to-do expropriated owners were paid below market prices; the nonnegotiable bonds given them as compensation bore interest at 3 percent initially and 1.5 percent later on; finally, not all expropriated owners have received the bonds, and none have ever been paid interest. Even if paid, the income would be one-sixth of their previous rents.

On the other hand, it has been pointed out that the tiny land holdings of less than one feddan still constitute 70 percent of the total number of properties, that there are two million farmers with less than one-half feddan, that the number of landless cultivators has increased, and, finally, that the number of new owners created by the redistributions stands in a very small ratio to the total number of farmers with insufficient land for a decent livelihood.

2. The shift from landless laborers to tenants, rising in one decade alone (1939–49) from 17 to 60 percent of the land. The difference in status—fundamentally that of a laborer in either case—was that the tenant enjoyed job security. This increase of security, indeed, has been called the chief gain of the land reform. In addition, however, tenants' share in agricultural value-added has risen by one-third, while the share of absentee owners has fallen by half.

3. Peasant welfare. During the Nasser regime, but particularly during the period before the Suez war, significant innovations have been made on behalf of peasant welfare. The so-called Gamoosa scheme, introduced in 1959, provided buffaloes "in calf" to cultivators on a hire-purchase basis; this is reportedly a very popular measure. A drinking water scheme provided clean water to the majority of villages. A striking innovation was the Combined Centers to provide health, educational, social, and agricultural services to the villages. As of 1964, 350 such centers served three-quarters of the rural population. The former heavy incidence of trachoma was greatly reduced; infant mortality fell in the districts served by the Centers.

4. Supervised Cooperatives. In conjunction with the land reforms, the government instituted, under the name of the Supervised Cooperatives, a new system of agriculture which constituted a new system of land management and—at the same time—an

---

[8] Hansen and Marzouk, *op. cit.*, p. 87. The figures pertain to 1963.

important vehicle for welfare measures. On the managerial side, to avoid the wasteful fragmentation of farming operations, the government allowed the beneficiaries of land distribution three strips of land divided among three fields over each of which the cooperative enforced a common crop and a uniform rotation. Thus the *fragmentation of ownership* resulting from the practices of inheritance and population increase was offset by an *amalgamation of operation*.

The system proved felicitous in several ways. For one thing, the typical savings of large-scale production were realized, such as common use of machinery, application of superior techniques, the use of skilled managers, etc. On the other hand, the individual peasant continued to own his plot and cultivate the land he owned. To offset the fact that the agricultural yield came at each harvest all in one crop, the peasants bartered one type of product for the others they required. Yields rose over the period 1952 to 1959 by 45 percent, in comparison to an average for all Egypt of 15 percent.

Aside from the gain in productivity, welfare aims could be served. When the Supervised Cooperatives took over the marketing of services, profits were allocated among reserves (40 percent), dividends (30 percent), the fund for sickness, accident insurance, and medical care (20 percent), and the members' refund share on sales (10 percent). There was a certain amount of forced saving in the system; but its advantages for the administration of rural welfare were patent. Latterly the system has been extended to villages not involved in land distributions. The element of government supervision was attenuated as the farmers learned to manage their own affairs. In this respect, and in the facts of private ownership and incomes depending on private productivity, the system differed clearly from collective farming in Communist countries.

We return to the subject of Egyptian agriculture in a subsequent discussion of the foreign trade deficit and the question as to whether agricultural production could help substantially in this problem.

In Egypt, the peasant has not profited appreciably from the growth of agricultural production, chiefly because population has increased at no less a rate. The rise of money wages has been cancelled out by inflation, particularly in the last decade; real wages did not rise over the whole span of years from 1950 to 1966 by more than 7 percent, an annual average of less than .5 percent.

A moot question regarding agricultural labor in Egypt is whether or not there exists a surplus supply. Economists of high standing disagree diametrically.[9] In the opinion of the present writer, economists upholding the surplus view are not necessarily maintaining that the subtraction of marginal laborers would not reduce output, but only that output would be reduced by less than a laborer's subsistence. Where family members are a part of the labor force of the farm and they share its joint output, as in Egypt, this is quite possible since it is only necessary that that joint output provide enough, when *averaged* over the family, to provide for their subsistence. Surplus labor then implies that the laborer is being given more (i.e., subsistence) than he produced

---

[9] The government has always spoken of a surplus, as though no doubt existed. Professor Hansen has taken a negative position, recently supported by a painstaking statistical inquiry, "Employment and Wages in Rural Egypt," *American Economic Review*, June 1969, pp. 298–313. But Donald C. Mead, in an equally impressive statistical study, concludes that surplus labor not only exists in Egyptian agriculture but will continue: cf., *Growth and Structural Changes in the Egyptian Economy* (Homewood, Illinois: Richard D. Irwin, Inc., 1967), pp. 80–98. Most writers believe surplus labor to be characteristic of underdeveloped economies in general.

as the marginal member of a group. General observation of rural labor in under-developed countries makes this appear to be a highly probable situation.

Industry

The second portion of the present chapter on Egypt, devoted to the evolution of the economy as a whole, also included a review of the course of industrial growth from Muhammad Ali through the nationalization of the sixties. Successive sections now are concerned with theoretical and practical issues in the evolution of Egyptian industry, including government policy; with a general view of its present complexion; and, thirdly, with an evaluation of its accomplishments.

Issues and Policies

Theories of economic development framed with special reference to the poorer economies usually posit that early progress in industrialization begins (and should begin) with the elaboration of native raw materials. In this respect Egypt is typical. During the decade 1945–54 approximately three-fifths of the increase of industrial production took place in the category "food, drink, and tobacco" and in spinning and weaving. Even the balance of industry was largely engaged in construction materials, such as cement and bricks. All of these draw on domestic raw produce, where clearly comparative advantages lie because of transportation costs.

But as Mead points out, Egypt departs from the conventional model of the developing country in that its foreign trade is not especially marked by import substitution, that is, the replacement of imports with substitutes produced domestically. There was of course some substitution. But if imports increase, as they did in the Egyptian case, no more than proportionally to the increase of total demand as indicated by GNP, it would be artificial to regard the limited growth of imports as a consequence of substitution. Their volume was held down, rather, by a simple lack of availability during the war and subsequently by exchange control. The result was "a remarkably diversified industrial sector, with a significant amount of output in a wide range of products, both producers goods and consumers goods."[10] This does not, of course, deny that some newer commodities such as automobile tires and certain consumers goods came to be uneconomically produced under a shield of protective tariffs.

Egypt departs also from another theoretical model, the theory of "balanced growth," promulgated principally by Ragnar Nurkse, according to which expansion of *supplies*, if it conforms to relative consumer choices, creates general expansion, each commodity constituting *demand* for the others. But if demand clearly leads over supply, as both Hansen and Mead believe to be typical of Egypt, the theory is not realized. Demand will be satisfied by imports until home production is encouraged by protection and the availability of capital.[11]

To turn now from the theoretical to actual practice, we find that Egypt began to practice industrial protection as soon as it achieved tariff autonomy in 1930. The chief items protected were cotton fabrics, cement, matches, sugar, alcohol, and cigarettes. With the passage of time, the list was extended, and the level of protection became very high: in 1952, 69.9 percent; in 1959, 130.9; and in 1961, 113.6 on imports other than

---

[10] Mead, *op. cit.*, pp. 102–05.
[11] Hansen and Marzouk, *op. cit.*, p. 149.

capital goods, raw materials, and "essential" consumers goods. Egyptian protective tariffs are said, on the authority of a United Nations report in 1954, to afford an example of infant industry protection in the sense that a significant list (including minerals, fertilizers, vegetable oils, soap, leather products, cigarettes, some processed foods, and, in certain respects, textiles) could dispense with protection. Many customs duties have been lowered; but, if the government so desires, complete protection can be achieved through direct controls and import licensing.

In addition to tariff protection, as we have noted previously, the government gave very substantial financial aid to industry through cheap loans and extensive participation in ownership by the Bank Misr and later by the expanded Misr Group. Other devices included bulk purchases, subsidies, and pricing policies on industrial goods. In the case of cotton textiles, the government gives direct subsidies and indirect support by the prices set on raw cotton by the Egyptian Cotton Commission, and by the requirement that the domestic mills use home-produced raw cotton, which is generally a longer staple and therefore relatively expensive. Because this requirement raises also the domestic price of cotton fabrics, it can in no sense be regarded as a welfare measure. Finally, beginning in the 1930s monopoly has been encouraged by the state in a variety of ways, including tariffs, which give 100 percent protection in the case of food, textiles, and building materials, and government ownership in other cases extending to 60 percent or more of industrial output since the nationalizations of 1961 and 1963.

Egyptian Industrial Production Including Electricity

Year	Index 1	Year	Index 1	Index 2	Year	Index 1	Index 2	Year	Index 2
1936	48	1950	98		1956	122	105	1962	174
1945	67	1951	97		1957	130	122	1963	200
1946	68	1952	100		1958	144	130	1964	219
1947	74	1953	101		1959	148	141	1965	237
1948	83	1954	106	102	1960	161	157		
1949	93	1955	115	104	1961	179	167		

Sources: Index 1: Hansen and Marzouk, *op cit.*, Table 5.2, p. 115 (1952=100). This index, set together from several series, is considered best by the authors.

Index 2: Ministry of Statistics, UAR, *Statistical Handbook 1952–1965*, p. 74 (1953 = 100). The different bases of these two indices cannot be disturbing since the change in value from 1952 to 1953 is slight.

Present Condition of Industry

The upshot of market and government forces on the development of industry in Egypt since the second world war is shown in the preceding table. The average rates of industrial growth corresponding to these figures are quite high: for the period 1939–62, 5 percent; for 1950–54, 2.5 percent; for 1955–62, 8 percent; for First Five Year Plan, 1960–end of 1964, 8 percent.

So far as concerns the relative annual growth rates of industry and agriculture, these are, for the period 1959–60 to 1964–65, 3.3 and 8.5 percent respectively.[12] It

[12] These figures and those for the service sectors referred to later are taken from Bent Hansen, "Planning and Economic Growth in Egypt, 1960–1965," in P. J. Vatikiotis (ed.), *Egypt Since the Revolution* (London: Allen and Unwin, 1968), p. 31.

may be well to bear in mind, as Professor Issawi points out, that the share of industry relative to agriculture and its rate of growth is artificially inflated by two factors: the much heavier and increasing degree of protection granted to industry, and the high and rising level of indirect taxation on manufactured goods.[13]

Beside the growth rates of industry, there are other attributes which are equally significant for an evaluation of "Arab Socialism," indeed in the aggregate more important. These include matters of productivity, employment, wages, and the like. Regarding productivity, doubtless the most critical element from the angle of economic development, Hansen has supplied some illuminating analysis, unfortunately not brought up to date. Productivity per person employed as well as per hour worked have both approximately doubled from 1937 to 1960, the greater part of the increase coming since 1947. Because of the low complement of capital with which each laborer works, perhaps one-fourth as much as, for example, in Sweden, the *absolute* level of productivity is low. The rate of increase of labor productivity in Egypt has evolved as follows: at 1 percent per person employed from 1937–47, 4.2 percent from 1947–60, 3.5 percent from 1952–60. In view of the fallibility of basic statistical information in Egypt (and the Middle East generally), the drop in productivity calculated for the eight years following the Revolution may not be accurate. More seriously, the rate of improvement of labor productivity ceased or declined from 1959–60 to 1962–63 despite a threefold increase of industrial investment.[14]

Less favorable evolutions characterize the course of wages, as pointed out earlier— a rise in real terms of 32 percent over ten years. Meanwhile the share of wages in total output at one-third is not only strikingly low compared to developed countries where the proportion may run from two-thirds to three-fourths, but is said to be declining during the past decade. The employment record is better: for manufacturing, a rise from 353,000 to 713,000 from 1937 to 1960, to 825,000 in 1965.[15]

The Value of Egyptian Industrialization

Some adverse judgments concerning the Egyptian industrialization program turn out on careful thought to be biased. Thus it has been said that "high prices and direct public assistance financed the country's industrial expansion, at the expense of the citizen, whether as consumer or taxpayer."[16] Of course, *any* investment in industry has to be financed through the prices of products of private enterprise or through taxes or subsidies for government undertakings. The real issue is one of cost-benefit. If the Egyptian per capita real income could have increased over the period 1945–60 (total real income rose by 4 percent annually while population increased by 2) *without* industrial expansion, it would be interesting to know what did account for it.

It has also been said that industrialization will not solve the problem of overpopulation. Undoubtedly this is true, but neither will any other purely economic action. This leads to the fairly "commonsense" conclusion that the birth rate is not significantly an economic problem, but a cultural, sociological, and religious matter.

[13] Issawi, *op. cit.*, p. 47, fn. 2.
[14] Hansen and Marzouk, *op. cit.*, pp. 129–35.
[15] For 1937 and 1960, Department of Statistics and Census figures adjusted by Mead, *op. cit.*, p. 111; for 1965, unadjusted figure, *Statistical Handbook 1952–1965*, p. 212.
[16] Kurt Grunwald and Joachim Ronall, *Industrialization in the Middle East* (New York: Council for Middle East Affairs Press, 1950), p. 202.

On the negative side, Egyptian industrialization probably erred in the emphasis on steel and iron (specifically regarding the Helwan complex), in its preoccupation with large-scale firms and undertakings, and in its reliance upon protection and monopoly. But on the positive side, it is not easy to assess the relative responsibilities for future development of agriculture and industry, which currently just about divide honors from the aggregative angles. Outside this plane of discourse, industry supplies somewhat more free savings than agriculture, and it would probably enjoy domestic markets which expand more as per capita incomes rise. But agriculture enjoys the benefit of long-tested comparative international advantage in some agricultural products and intriguing possibilities of diversification in others. On the whole, a categoric choice scarcely seems to be justified at present.

The Service Sector

It would be an error to allow a preoccupation with the relative promise of agriculture and industry to lead to a neglect of the quantitatively much less impressive sector of the services, which may, however, have great strategic importance. Certain service industries achieved extraordinarily high rates of annual increase during the period of the First Plan (1959–60 to 1964–65): electricity and public utilities, 18.0 percent; construction, 10.4 percent; and transport and communications, 11.1 percent.

Not only are these sectors notable for high rates, but also for the fact that they are essential bases of industrial and general economic growth. Construction carries with it additional significance in the interest shown by the government in low-cost housing.

With respect to transportation, before its closing in 1967 the Suez Canal accounted for 40 percent of the contribution to national income from this sector. Even when it is opened, the Canal will have to be dredged and widened to accommodate the new giant oil tankers. In some quarters the view is expressed that the oil trade will have become accustomed to alternative routes and will permanently desert the Suez route, while others hold that other freight and passengers will take the place of oil. If not, the fact that other Arab countries are now making good the loss of Suez revenue to Egypt by government contributions really affords cold comfort to that country because of the political uncertainties involved.

One aspect of the service sector appears problematical—the vast expansion of employment in personal and other services. From 1937 to 1960 the number thus employed doubled, a direct result of population pressure and threatening or overt unemployment in agriculture. In 1960, which may be typical, about 20 percent of the employment in the personal service category was accounted for in domestic service, often of a supernumerary character. But it was the state which bore the brunt of "making work," partly through the rule that any university graduate could find a job with the government if he chose. In the period 1947–60 government employment, even aside from government enterprises and nationalized firms, increased by half a million, or 40 percent of the new jobs opening up. Over the five years 1960–65 of the new Plan, another quarter million were thus accommodated.[17] The proliferation of government personnel is certainly one of the most acute problems of socialism as practiced in Egypt.

---

[17] Mead, *op. cit.*, pp. 131, 138–39; *Statistical Handbook*, 1964–65, p. 221.

Welfare

Population density and population increase are matters which imbue nearly all aspects of public welfare in Egypt. Although the great density is an old phenomenon because of a concentration of people in the valley and delta of the Nile, rates of increase were moderate until the censuses of 1947 and 1960 revealed rates of 1.8 and 2.5 per annum. The sudden change came from a fall in the death rate due to the spread of antibiotics, insecticides, and improved sanitation. The demographic problem can only be surmounted by a fall in the birth rate, and the government has taken some steps in this direction. But from a humane angle, further reduction in the death rate would be equally imperative. Such enervating parasitical diseases as amoebic infections, bilharzia, trachoma, and gastroenteritis are not amenable to antibiotics and can only be conquered by a combination of methods all of which involve costs, both private and public.

Poverty and unemployment are both in part functions of population pressure. The average worker had to provide for 25 percent more dependents in 1960 than in 1947; meanwhile, real wage rates had advanced in a smaller proportion. Employment in agriculture stagnated with an increase of less than 20 percent in the same period. As a consequence of low wages and rural unemployment, there has been a shift to the cities; it involved 750,000 persons in the decade 1937–47 and still continues at about the same rate. Thus rural unemployment is being transferred, as in most underdeveloped economies, to the cities. From 1947 to 1960 the official figures of unemployment grew in the provinces from 345,000 to 498,000 and in the urban portion, from 171,000 to 242,000.

In part, however, unemployment comes about through a lack of appropriate education and training. There is a plethora of university graduates but a shortage of trained managers, engineers, doctors, and the like. This imbalance has not yielded to a mere reduction of illiteracy, where significant advances have been made. Between the censuses of 1937 and 1960 illiteracy fell from 85.2 to 70.3 percent, a doubling of the decline registered in the previous 30 years; this was an essential element in economic development.

Egypt is well provided with labor legislation—we have noted some of these laws in passing. But a detailed account would scarcely prove rewarding as the plain facts are that trade unions are limited to large companies, and their bargaining power is weak; before 1962 workers were said to be at the mercy of their employers, and since the nationalizations, at the mercy of the state. With the advent of the revolution in 1952, strikes had been made illegal, and Professor Hansen observes that even in a socialist economy, "the manager will usually be interested in buying labor as cheaply as possible."[18] That no significant labor unrest became visible was in some degree attributable to the fact that industrial laborers frequently have come from the villages where wages are much lower. But in part it may be explained by the proverbial stoicism of the Egyptian common man.

Labor's share in national income has shown a tendency to fall; from 70 percent in 1939 it declined to 40 percent in 1952 and to about 35 percent in 1962. There is general agreement that Egyptian labor is inefficient because of poor health, illiteracy, and lack of training. For a time the low level of wages has more than compensated for the

---

[18] Hansen and Marzouk, *op. cit.*, p. 163.

21

inefficiency. While the average annual wage cost per unit of output rose over the years 1955–61 by three-quarters of 1 percent in the United States and by 3.5 percent in the United Kingdom, it fell in Egypt by 2.5 to 3.0 percent. Thus Egyptian labor improved its competitiveness internationally. But this development was probably reversed when, in connection with the nationalizations (1961–63), a serious wage-cost inflation was allowed to take place.

International Trade and Finance

The central fact of Egypt's international economic position is the deficit in its balance of payments. Save for three years, the deficit has prevailed since the second world war; it is a major preoccupation of economic policy now; and its evolution in the future is crucial to Egyptian development. Its magnitude over the sixties has varied between 1.2 and 7.2 percent of the gross domestic product. In absolute size it has fallen gradually from E£ 36.9 million in 1962 to the latest available figure, E£ 16.8 million in 1967. We shall be concerned with the question as to how these deficits came to pass, their significance in the total economic panorama, and what policies can remedy the situation.

What Has Caused the Deficits?

Balance-of-payments deficits are a common ailment of developing countries, and the commonest cause is domestic inflation, resting upon budgetary deficits and too open a hand in the granting of credit by commercial banks, resulting in an excessive creation of money. None of this applies to Egypt in any significant degree. Over the years 1949 to 1960, the wholesale price index rose by about 35 percent or 2.7 percent per annum, a very modest degree of inflation. Indeed, in view of the increase in gross national income at constant prices by 36.3 percent during these 11 years compared to an increase in the money supply by slightly less than 30 percent, there would have been a deflationary movement of prices if the public had not decreased its demand for money. Because one of the reasons for the monetary stability was price fixing and rationing on some consumers goods, there was excess demand in some markets; but the aggregative picture is clearly not one of much inflation. During the sixties inflationary pressures were aggravated by an increased annual increment to the money supply averaging 12 percent through 1967, compared to the previous average of not quite 3 percent. Even so, the general wholesale price index rose from 1961 through December 1968, by only 4.3 percent per annum, surely a small rate for a developing country.[19]

If inflation fails to explain the foreign deficit, could it not have been adverse developments in the underlying supply and demand conditions for exports and imports? This would appear to be plausible from the disaster which overtook the cotton market and Egypt's export values in the early fifties and the slow recovery thereafter. The income terms of trade, the real quality of imports which could be purchased from the proceeds of the country's exports, dropped by 40 percent from 1951 to 1952, and have risen only gradually since then; it seems probable that it was only in 1963 that they attained the 1950–51 levels.[20]

---

[19] National Bank of Egypt, *Economic Bulletin*, vol. xxii, No. 1, 1969.
[20] Mead, *op. cit.*, p. 165.

Quite possibly the setback to the terms of international trade had something to do with the size and persistence of Egypt's payments deficits, but the timing does not indicate this to be the major factor. In the first place, the deficits began with the end of the war in 1945, but the collapse of the cotton market did not come until 1952. Secondly, for a decade after 1952 there was a movement—fluctuating indeed, but with a fairly clear trend—toward a restoration of Egypt's former terms of trade, but the deficits increased, rather than declined.

What then does account for the phenomenal increase of Egyptian imports by 40 percent from the end of the war to 1959–60 and by an additional 30 percent in the following three years, despite a practically stagnant value of exports? The answer lies in the financing of the deficits by foreign capital. First came the utilizing of Egypt's sterling balances which had accumulated because of the military outlays by the United Kingdom during the second world war. The first releases of these frozen balances came in June 1947, followed by further sums in 1948 and subsequently, a process which reputedly put a considerable strain on the British economy. In any event, the sterling balances were sufficient not only to finance the Egyptian import surplus through 1958, but to permit an outflow of private capital and the acquisition of gold and other foreign assets. From 1959 on, the deficits were financed by loans and grants of foreign governments. Through 1966 these were chiefly American, in the form of loans and grants, totaling $925 million, including Public Law 480 shipments of wheat. This total economic aid equaled 40 percent of that extended to Turkey and 54 percent to Greece, but was larger by two-thirds than the aid given to Israel. From 1967, American aid to Egypt dwindled away and was supplanted by Soviet loans, currently thought to be the largest part of the Egyptian foreign debt.

Now that the real "cause" of the balance-of-payments deficits is revealed, it also becomes evident why inflation has been held in check in Egypt. In addition to domestic factors such as the growth of GNP and the expanded demand for money by the public, the inflow of goods from foreign loans has offset by so much the growth of money supply. Thus economic development can be had without tears. The rub comes if the flow of grants or loans declines and/or the service of existing debt begins to catch up with new credits, as it must unless they can be had at an accelerating rate. For this reason, the problem of mastering the deficit must be solved either by automatic and probably unwelcome reactions or by deliberately chosen policies.

Policies to Combat the Deficit

The range of choices does not seem to be manifold, at least for the near future. Although in the long run Egypt should be able to pay for its imports by "being able to produce at home a higher proportion of the intermediate and final goods needed for domestic uses . . . we can find little evidence that this stage is fast approaching," writes Donald Mead. To avoid a drop in the growth of output, there must be a substantial increase in the rate of saving.[21] In substance this is also the conclusion of Hansen. Ruling out the reduction of imports of capital goods, raw materials, and manufactured goods because they are essential to continued growth, the alternatives boil down to diminishing the imports of food or increasing exports; but the latter does not seem promising within the near future. So far as concerns raw cotton, even

---

[21] Mead, *op. cit.*, pp. 192, 225.

taking account of the results of the Aswan Dam, the cotton producing area can be expanded only by 6 percent, increasing the export of cotton by E£ 5–E£ 8 million, a mere drop in the bucket compared to the annual deficits in the balance of payments. And cotton textiles can, within the framework of the World Textiles Agreement, take care of only a minor portion of the gap. [22]

Thus the sole road is increased taxation to prevent an increase of per capita food consumption in order that most of the 20 percent increase in agricultural output expected from the Aswan Dam be left free to take the place of the food imports previously supported by foreign aid. Against this austere diagnosis is to be set the optimistic judgment that there is enough leeway in the fiscal system to compass the objective. In the first place, price subsidies could be abolished. Since the tax system bears more heavily on the rich than upon the poor, a tax on wealth can be recommended. Even after these measures, there will be no avoiding increases in food taxes, since these bear directly on the import surplus. To include also the consumption "in kind" on the farms, it will be necessary to introduce progressive taxation of agricultural incomes. In a socialist state, tax evasion should offer no problems! [23]

An Evaluation of Arab Socialism

International Comparisons [24]

Population grew in Egypt during 1968 at an estimated 2.7 percent per annum, the same rate as for the Near East as a whole. Gross national product for 1966 amounted to $168 per capita, the lowest in the Near East save for Yemen. But the *growth* rate of real gross domestic product at 5 to 6 percent over the years 1960–67 put the country in the same bracket as Iraq, Syria, and Turkey, above Lebanon in the 4-5 percent group and below Iran in the group of 6 percent or more. Egypt registered *growth* rates of gross *domestic* capital formation of 2.1 percent for 1955–60 and 2.3 percent for 1960–65, near the lower limit of the 54 countries included in the United Nations category of developing areas. Gross domestic capital formation at 15 percent of gross domestic product in both periods occupied a median position in the same array of countries.

During the first and second halves of the decade 1955–65, while Egypt was showing rates of increase of gross domestic product of 4.5 and 5.2 percent respectively—about median values for the 54 developing countries—agriculture grew at 4 and 3 percent, again a typical rate; while industry grew at 14 and 16 percent, the highest recorded rates of all the countries; and while exports increased at 7 and 5 percent, again something like a median rate. Over the decade 1958–67, the cost of living rose by 31 percent, a very low rate, indeed, among the developing countries.

Aside from these rather cold aggregative figures, it may be rewarding to summarize the record of economic development in Egypt as it appears from the evidence of the preceding pages and the evaluations expressed there on specific points by a number of economists.

---

[22] Hansen and Marzouk, *op. cit.*, pp. 240–43; 272–73.

[23] Bent Hansen, *Economic Development in Egypt*, Research Program on Economic and Political Problems and Prospects of the Middle East, the RAND Corporation, RM–5961–FF, October 1969.

[24] The sources of the comparisons are: United Nations: *World Economic Survey 1967*, Part I, and United States AID, *Economic Data Book: Near East and South Asia*, December 1968, and World Bank, *Annual Reports*. Figures given for the UAR do not always correspond to those utilized in the preceding pages, but are cited here for the sake of the comparisons.

Unfavorable Aspects

Disuse and Misuse of the Price System

This feature of the present Egyptian economic system is considered by a number of competent observers to be its worst flaw. On the score of *disuse*, many of the errors of planning and its inefficiency arise from this source. Furthermore, the failure to exploit the automatic working of market forces is in part responsible for an unwieldy bureaucracy which is also the subject of widespread criticism. That socialism does not preclude extensive reliance on the price system has been demonstrated theoretically by a number of distinguished economists; and the experience of Yugoslavia and other Communist countries has afforded a practical demonstration of the same fact.

The *misuse* of the price system is visible in the "shortage economy," involving rationing, queues, and lack of consumer sovereignty. The whole field of foreign trade on both the export and import sides is characterized by arbitrary rules and decisions and internal inconsistencies—drawbacks which appear specifically in the field of infant industry protection.

Both the disuse and misuse of the price system may result in part from the relative novelty of socialism and planning in Egypt.

Bureaucracy

During the period of the first Five Year Plan alone the outlay for civilian administration grew from 5 to 10 percent of GNP. This tendency, called "the most serious problem in the development of the Egyptian economy," results partly from the use of government positions as a method of unemployment relief, and partly from making economic governance too extensively a matter of authoritarian decisions in the place of market forces.

Preoccupation With Manufacturing

Not to deny the appropriateness of industrialization, it must nevertheless be said that the construction of plant and other physical industrial facilities has, in appreciable measure, come at the cost of investments for improving and expanding the supply of skilled artisans, engineers, production managers, and the like. Scarcity of these inputs has been a severe bottleneck in productive capacity.

The Demographic Problem

The inhabited part of Egypt (the Nile Valley) has long been one of the most densely populated regions in the world, with 650 persons to the square mile, compared to 288 in Belgium, 214 in the United Kingdom, and 213 in West Germany. Furthermore, over the years 1958 to 1969, the population has grown from over 24 million to over 32 million, i.e., by one third! Despite the neutrality of the Islamic culture on the question of birth control, the government has dallied but is now reputed to be considering an appeal for mass sterilization of males.[25] Engineering triumphs such as the Aswan High Dam can be nullified in a brief span by the flood of new consumers.

---

[25] *Los Angeles Times*, September 25, 1969.

Wars

Finally, in a list of economic evils comes perhaps the greatest—the cost of the military establishment. Even in 1965, not a war year, this cost amounted to a tenth of the GNP. Economic development in Egypt, in the sense of per capita income and all that this barren figure means in human welfare, depends primarily upon two non-economic forces, the cultural matter of population, and the political matter of peace and war.

Favorable Aspects

Possessed of power without significant opposition within the country, the revolutionary government has, in general, used it for social purposes. The distribution of wealth and income has become less unequal, though extremes of poverty and wealth still exist. In some fields, as for example in the civil service, the marked reduction of unequal incomes may indeed have gone so far as to impair incentive; but in general, personal incomes are left to supply and demand forces.

There is virtual agreement that the rate of growth of income at an average rate between 5 and 6 percent per annum is impressive, as indeed also is the increased rate of investment from 12 to 18 percent from 1959–60 to 1962–63. Furthermore, this has been done without a particularly disturbing rate of inflation. Of course the growth rates were achieved, in the last analysis, on the basis of economic wherewithal supplied from abroad, and it is unlikely that the inflow of foreign capital realized in the decade 1957 to 1967 will endure. But the Egyptian economy has been set upon an upward course which could be maintained without foreign capital by sufficiently rational and firm policies.

We have observed that the low level of wages in Egypt is not altogether nullified by equally low efficiency, with the result that a competitive edge in costs exists in international markets in some fields.

So far as concerns Egyptian planning, a distinctive feature has been its operation through the central regulation of saving and investment, while day-to-day operations are in principle left to local and plant managers. This decentralization is potentially a source of economic strength; but the bureaucratic forces are strong, and latterly the tendency has been reported to be toward the spread of centralized functions.

In conclusion, it will be well to remember that, as Professor Charles Issawi points out, Egypt is Islamic, a religion which is "one of the best equipped (among oriental religions) to cope with both economic development and cultural modernization. Islam is basically a rational, positive, equalitarian, and non-ritualistic religion. . . . In certain ways, such as its attitude toward birth control and its respect for commercial activity, it is particularly conducive to economic development."

II. IRAQ: IS OIL ENOUGH?

Brief Political Retrospect

The turbulent internal and international history of Iraq during the past half century is explicable at least in part as the result of national pride and nationalism, rooted in a remote but glorious past, now confronted by strong religious, political, and regional differences. From the eighth century, when Arab armies defeated the Persian rulers, until the end of the thirteenth century, when the country was overrun by the Mongols, Baghdad was the center of the world's leading civilization. Some 15 to 18 million people then lived in an area which supported only one and a half million a century ago. Parts of the irrigation system from the heyday of ancient Mesopotamia are still in use.[1] But the boundaries of present-day Iraq were drawn arbitrarily by the great powers at the end of the first world war, and the Kurds in the mountainous northern region have remained a dissident element.

The Mongols were succeeded in 1534 by the Ottoman Turks under Sulaiman the Magnificent, and the country remained under Turkish rule until the first world war. In April 1920, Iraq was awarded to Great Britain as a mandated territory, precipitating an uprising with a considerable cost of life on both sides. Subsequent Anglo-Iraqi treaties proclaimed the country to be a sovereign state under King Faisal I (1920) and as fully independent (1930). All special political ties with Britain ended in 1955, and the Hashemite kingdom (so-called after the reigning family), terminated with the Kassem military coup of July 14, 1958.

During the period from 1920 to 1958 there were some 58 cabinets, marked by shifts within the ruling cliques of army, religious authorities, and quasi-feudal sheiks—the large landowners—whom the British had supported as a means of preserving order. Until 1958, the government under the conservative Prime Minister Nuri al-Said vigorously suppressed Communist movements (1947, 1949, and 1952–53), aligning itself with the Western democracies, especially the United States, and joining the Baghdad Pact with Turkey, Iran, Pakistan, and Great Britain in 1955. However, the domestic opposition, led by certain army officers and young intellectuals, became increasingly hostile toward the West, favoring in theory an espousal of Arabism and international

---

[1] Kathleen M. Langley, *The Industrialization of Iraq*, Harvard Middle Eastern Monographs V (Cambridge: Harvard University Press, 1961), introduction.

political neutrality. In practice, after the revolution of 1958, this spelled the beginning of a withdrawal from the Western sphere of influence and, instead, sympathy for the policies of Gamal Abdel Nasser.[2] The latter tendency encountered strong, and sometimes violent, internal dissent.

The decade of the sixties was marked by a five-year guerrilla war with the Kurds, ending in 1966; by frequent cabinet changes; by several coups which displaced presidents and premiers; and by the breaking of diplomatic relations with the United States, Great Britain, and West Germany in June 1967 following charges by the United Arab Republic that America aided Israel in the war.

The recent economic history of Iraq falls into three periods: from the beginning of the British mandate in 1920 to the great increase in oil exports in 1950; from 1950 to the revolution of July 14, 1958; and from the revolution to the present. The dividing lines between these periods are both political and economic.

Economic Development Prior to the Plans, 1920–50

During these three decades Iraq experienced some economic development, particularly in physical plants, but the rate of development was slow. Thus between 1933 and 1950, the government did devote a significant fraction of its expenditures to capital projects, rarely falling below one-tenth and for the latter part of the thirties running between one-fourth and one-third. But the fraction during the forties had fallen back to the level of the early thirties. For this lack of consistent progress, a combination of factors was responsible.[3] On the political side, Iraq was troubled with domestic dissent by the Kurds, Bedouin tribes and the like, and by disturbed relations with Britain, the problem of the Palestinian refugees, and the second world war. Although the constitution provided for a cabinet form of government following the British model, the country lacked a responsible party system to put the system into effect. Furthermore, as nearly always happens when a foreign nation controls, the long years of Turkish domination had failed to raise up a corps of able civil servants and administrators. With the exception of King Faisal I (1921–33), the government lacked imagination and drive.

Economically, Iraq during the decades from 1920–50 suffered from the ubiquitous lack of capital afflicting all developing economies (shortly to be remedied!) and the similarly widespread lack of skilled laborers and technicians which persists to the present day. Sharing further in the common complaint of developing countries, the government was handicapped by inadequate revenues. The peasant class was too poor to supply much tax revenue, and the rich landowners were politically too powerful to brook significant taxation. The residual legatees, the urban workers, both private and government, could not be burdened with an income tax sufficient to provide an adequate public revenue.

As might be expected from these facts, the three decades prior to 1950 are not attractive from an economic angle, though they do bear witness to the significance of petroleum for the nation. Until 1934 crude oil production was unimportant, rarely exceed-

---

[2] Royal Institute of International Affairs, *op. cit.*, pp. 241–52.
[3] The following analysis is based upon Fahim I. Qubain, *The Reconstruction of Iraq, 1950–1957* (New York: Frederick A. Praeger, Inc., 1958), pp. 22–28.

ing 100 thousand tons annually. From that figure in one bound it rose to one million in 1934, with the completion of pipelines from Kirkuk to Haifa and Tripoli, to over three million the next year, and to more than four million in 1937 and 1938. The war cut into oil exports for the next three years, after which annual production came to exceed four million tons for the balance of the forties. The sudden increase to six and eight million tons per annum in 1950 and 1951 ushered in a period of acceleration, not only of oil production, but of economic development.

Prior to this upsweep, oil production and the economy grew slowly and irregularly but unmistakably through the joint action of domestic outlays by the oil companies and in larger measure through oil revenues paid to the government. Save for the war years, 1941–45, there is a fairly steady rise in government capital formation, paralleling the increase of oil revenues. Undoubtedly, part of the non-oil government revenue also can be ascribed to this industry through multiplier effects of its expenditures in the economy.

Government Revenue and Capital Works 1934–49
(in millions of Iraqi dinars)

Year	Total revenue	Oil revenue	Capital works	Year	Total revenue	Oil revenue	Capital works
1934	5.02	1.02	.42	1942	13.83	1.56	.98
1935	5.36	.59	1.03	1943	18.10	1.88	1.65
1936	6.03	.60	2.18	1944	18.89	2.22	0.00
1937	6.94	.73	2.37	1945	20.22	2.32	1.54
1938	7.84	1.98	2.46	1946	25.10	2.33	3.05
1939	9.21	2.02	2.23	1947	26.02	2.35	3.57
1940	9.72	1.58	2.71	1948	26.72	2.01	3.93
1941	10.16	1.46	.96	1949	28.63	3.24	3.38

Source: Qubain, *op. cit.*, pp. 21, 31.

Rapid Development, 1950–58

General Characteristics

During these years "Iraq entered an era of accelerated economic and social development which had no parallel in the history of the country since the golden age of the Abbassid Caliphate some twelve centuries ago."[4] It would, of course, be an error to ascribe the initiation of this era to oil production alone, since part of the story belongs in the realm of ideas—the cumulative effect of several decades of growing materialistic aspirations. Economic development could not, however, occupy the center of the stage in the formative years of the independent country during the thirties, nor in the war nor during the preoccupation with the Palestinian question after the war. But there can be little doubt that the phenomenal wave of oil output which followed the completion of a complementary 16-inch pipeline to Tripoli in 1949 triggered an economic upswing which was sustained by uninterrupted increases of oil production through the next five years.

[4] *Ibid.*, p. 30.

29

Simultaneously with the great increase of petroleum production, economic planning was inaugurated in Iraq with the creation of a Development Board in 1950 and the launching of a six-year program in 1951. The original law allocated to development the entire flow of oil royalties to the government; but two years later, because of the expanding functions of government and the attending budgetary load, 30 percent was thenceforth to go to ordinary budget purposes, leaving 70 percent for development. Even so, from the fiscal year 1951–52 through fiscal 1953–54, the allotment of funds to the Development Board exceeded by approximately twofold its actual expenditures. This is scarcely surprising in view of the time inevitably required for formulating plans and recruiting staff.

In 1953 a new law was enacted concerning the Development Board which deprived it of its political autonomy by placing it under a Ministry of Development. In part this change arose from the fact that employees of the board, being outside the civil service status, received higher salaries; resentment was intensified by the fact also that the board's budget exceeded that of the regular government; and finally, its projects were geared to long-range economic growth, bringing only small immediate gains to the population generally.

By 1955, before the first plan had run its course, a new program was presented to the Parliament, partly to take account of the rapid increase of oil revenues, which had evolved as shown in the following table. After the passage of a year, a modified pro-

Government Revenues, Total and from Oil, 1950–58
(in millions of Iraqi dinars)

Year	Total	Oil	Year	Total	Oil	Year	Total	Oil
1950	33.49	5.28	1953	47.72	51.34	1956	124.88	69.0
1951	37.53	13.93	1954	52.17	68.37	1957	114.84	49.0
1952	50.54	37.63	1955	65.28	73.74	1958	97.72	84.6

Source: Qubain, *op. cit.*, pp. 21, 31; Langley, *op. cit.*, p. 303, and United Nations, *Statistical Yearbooks.*

gram for six years, 1955–60, was put into effect. It differed from the plan of the previous quinquennium in important respects.[5] Its rate of planned expenditures amounted to ID 85 million annually, in place of the ID 31 million of the first plan. It was more decentralized in control. It was presented to the Parliament in tentative form, subject to subsequent revision. In the sphere of agriculture, emphasis was shifted from flood control to irrigation, drainage, and reclamation, since the problem of floods had largely been surmounted. More importance was given to improving transportation facilities—both railroad and highway—because of the realization that increased production is pointless without an adequate marketing mechanism. Industry received a higher priority than before. And finally, the "new-factory syndrome" of the first plan was offset by giving attention to the better use of existing plant.

The spirit of optimism, progress, and endeavor which permeated the leadership of Iraq during these years led to a number of important visits to the country by expert

[5] *Ibid.*, pp. 45–48.

groups and an equal number of economic reports.[6] All of these reports cautioned against trying to force the pace of industrialization too rapidly. The International Bank warned against creating inefficient industries. Professor Iversen laid great emphasis upon developing agriculture, although in the very long run industry would be important. Lord Salter pointed out that Iraq's oil royalties would mean that most industrial products would be advantageously imported. According to the Little report, it would be an error to produce items unless their cost was less than that of imports. In general, as the following survey of economic sectors shows, the economic policies of the government and the recommendations of the Development Board followed the general course recommended by these reports.

Expenditures of the Iraq Development Board

Item	Actual expenditures 1951–56		Allocated expenditures 1951–56		Actual expenditures		
					1956–57	1957–58 [1]	
	IDm.	%	IDm.	%	IDm.	IDm.	%
Administration	1.3	1.6	3.2	2.0	n.a.	1.8	3.8
Irrigation and reclamation	37.3	45.0	70.8	45.7	n.a.	10.0	21.1
Roads and bridges	17.9	21.6	26.8	17.2	n.a.	9.0	19.0
Buildings	13.9	16.7	18.0	11.6	n.a.	19.2	40.5
Industries	5.4	6.5	31.1	20.0	n.a.	7.5	15.8
Other	7.3	8.8	5.4	3.5	n.a.	.0	.0
Total expenditure	83.1	100.0	155.4	100.0	45.0	47.5	100.0
Total revenue	168.3				51.0	36.0	

[1] Estimated.

Source: *Quarterly Bulletin of the Central Bank of Iraq*, July–September 1957, and *Economic Developments in the Middle East, 1957–1958* (New York: United Nations, 1959), given in Langley, *op. cit.*, p. 172.

It will be observed that the board allocated nearly all of its revenues during the first Six Year Plan, 1951–56; but that its actual expenditures were only about one-half of its revenues. During the first two years of the second Six Year Plan, annual revenues fell off from the level achieved in 1955–56, which was ID 60.8 millions (not shown on the table). No doubt for this reason, expenditures came closer to revenue in 1956–57; and in 1957–58, when the closure of the pipeline through Syria occurred, expenditures exceeded revenue. The table also shows how greatly agriculture exceeded any other allocation of expenditures in the first plan and how it declined in relative importance in 1957–58.

---

[6] IBRD, *The Economic Development of Iraq* (Baltimore, Md.: The Johns Hopkins Press, 1952); J. H. White Engineering Corporation, *Report to Iraq Development Board* (Baghdad: mimeographed, 1954); Carl Iversen, *A Report on Monetary Policy in Iraq* (Copenhagen: Eljnar Munksgaard, Publishers, 1954); Lord Salter, *The Development of Iraq: A Plan of Action* (London: Iraq Development Board, 1955); Arthur D. Little, Inc., "A Plan for Industrial Development of Iraq," mimeographed (Cambridge, Mass., 1956).

Agriculture

Let us first examine the main characteristics of agriculture in Iraq, turning later to government policies and their successes and shortcomings in this field in the period 1950–58. What are the resources and products of this sector of economic life, what are its chief economic problems, what record does it show in productivity?

Reviewing the general situation in 1955, the Danish economist, Professor Carl Iversen, painted a gloomy picture, relieved only by the possibility of future improvement. Per capita income had been estimated by the United Nations in 1949, prior to the appearance of any domestic figures, at $85 per annum. Sixty percent of the population drew their livelihood from agriculture. But only a third of the cultivable land was utilized, and of that, one-third lay fallow. The agricultural sector was marked by underemployment; methods of cultivation were woefully primitive and inefficient.[7] An English visitor, Professor Critchley, wrote that it was "not exaggeration to state that the average agricultural worker is a living pathological specimen" as he was probably a victim of hookworm, intestinal roundworm, malaria, schistosomiasis, trachoma, bejel, and possibly also tuberculosis. In certain rural areas, infant mortality ran to 300–500 per thousand!

Part of the explanation for this state of affairs, lies in a hostile natural environment and part in human institutions. In contrast to the benevolence of the Nile, which supplies enriching silt and an abundance of water for the planting season, the Tigris and Euphrates have steep gradients which flush the silt into a marshy delta, producing floods along the way, especially in the spring when crops are being planted. In the upper parts of the valley, salinity results from aridity and high temperatures; in the lower or southern part, it results from capillary action which carries salt upward from a stratum extending under the sea. One commission has reported that 20–30 percent of the cultivated land in some areas had been abandoned in the course of three decades because of salination, which could be remedied by proper drainage. Hence, major preoccupations of the government have been flood control, irrigation, and drainage.

On the score of institutions, the outstanding feature until recently has been the extreme inequality in land ownership. In the decade of the fifties, reliable and complete statistical evidence is lacking, but it is said on good authority that 68 percent of owners held only 8 percent of the land, and that 67 percent of the land fell into holdings exceeding 620 acres.[8] For all practical purposes, the country lacked a small peasant proprietor class; most of the land was held by tribal sheiks and wealthy city capitalists. Characteristically the sharecropper, who actually worked the land, received 40 percent of the crop after a tenth had been taken by the government and 50 percent by the landowner and his agents.

The main concern of the Development Board, established in 1950, was directed toward the physical side of agricultural development, mainly the control and use of water in the great Tigris-Euphrates valley. During the first Six Year Plan, 1951–56, the emphasis was put upon flood control; in the second Six Year Plan, 1956–61, the effort was shifted toward irrigation and drainage. Outstanding accomplishments were the Tharthar flood control scheme on the Tigris and the Habbaniya flood-control and irrigation system on the Euphrates, both inaugurated in April 1956. During the

---

[7] Iversen, *op. cit.*, pp. 69–71.
[8] Royal Institute of International Affairs, *op. cit.*, p. 257; Qubain, *op. cit.*, p. 86.

decade of the fifties, the total outlay was estimated at ID 180 million ($504 million), substantially completing the irrigation part of the project. Undoubtedly this represented the largest program in the Middle East, adding nearly a million acres to the arable land of Iraq.

The program of the Development Board has been severely criticized as too much devoted to the physical aspects of agriculture, as an exclusively "engineers' approach" to development, leaving the people out of consideration. "In the past, Iraq was poor because its people could not master their environment. Today Iraq is poor because it has more money than it can invest; and the reason this is so is that the social structure is not adapted to expansion." [9] While abstractly there is much force in this criticism, it is necessary to realize that adapting the social structure to expansion is not a matter of a few years' effort, nor did it lie within the powers of the Development Board to do so. There can be little doubt that agriculture and not industry required primary emphasis, nor that flood control, irrigation, and drainage were eligible projects for large investments making a real long-run contribution toward development. Probably these activities were relatively overdone, compared to imaginable less-costly alternatives with a shorter-run yield period. But with the immense flood of oil revenues accruing to the board after 1950, it is easy to understand its bias toward the large projects actually chosen.

Turning from physical to institutional matters, land tenure presents the chief problem in Iraqi farming. When the Turks left the country, they took with them or destroyed the records of land registry; in consequence legal evidences of ownership disappeared. There ensued a chaotic period of uncertainty and dispute, during which the government laboriously undertook a cadastral survey, beginning in 1933. In the shuffle, the tribal chieftains and other persons of affluence succeeded in establishing ownership rights, dispossessing the actual cultivators. To make matters worse, a law of 1933 provided that if a sharecropper was dismissed or moved from a plantation, he must pay all debts to his landlord, failing which he was forbidden employment by any other plantation, government office, private business, or domestic service. Finally, the large landowners were the most powerful class in the country, socially and politically. They paid no taxes on their property and the income tax was not progressive.

In this situation, land reform in the sense of a redistribution from the rich to the poor was impossible without a revolution (which finally did occur). Fortunately, however, the government was the owner of 60 percent of the land; "it outflanked the problem [of unequal ownership] and took the line of least resistance, namely the distribution of government land with assisted development and a variety of other governmental aids." [10] Accordingly, by laws enacted in 1945, 1951, and 1952, plots of public land of stipulated sizes were to be given without charge to the landless inhabitants of the area and to graduates of agricultural schools, retired army and police personnel, and government employees. To acquire full title, the tenant had to occupy the land for ten years and cultivate it according to instructions, being obliged also to build a house according to specifications, and to participate in a cooperative scheme of marketing and consumption. Government loans up to ID 100 were available at 3 percent. All of the allocated land was to be incorporated into a "settlement."

---

[9] Warriner, *op. cit.*, pp. 116–21.
[10] Qubain, *op. cit.*, p. 90.

Between 1945 and 1955, 1.7 million acres (to be compared to the one million acres made arable by irrigation and drainage) were distributed, about one-fifth of which were accompanied by government supervision and planning. Of the settlements, the one on the Dujailah canal, founded in 1945, is the best known and largest, which had a population in 1955 of 14,320 persons, served by primary and secondary education facilities, health clinics, agricultural demonstration centers, and small industries. In 1955 some 80,000 persons lived in the settlements.

Other lines of government activity on behalf of agriculture in the fifties were farm mechanization, agricultural credit, agricultural extension, research and training, the cooperative movement, and crop diversification. All of these were promising, but they constituted merely a formative stage.

A retrospect over the period 1950–58 shows that agriculture was the most important sphere of economic activity of the government, and the only one of comparable magnitude in the Middle East. Flood control was essential to the safety and health of the population; irrigation and drainage greatly expanded the arable land, a justifiable investment from a long-run viewpoint. If popularity of the Development Board and the government were the principal aim, more attention to short-run gains in the standard of living and welfare of the mass of people would have been wise; but the difficulty of using the large oil revenues effectively on short notice should be recognized. From both the long- and short-run viewpoints, the land distributions seem to be amply warranted.

Since the product of agriculture is variable because of seasonal influences, comparisons involving two dates are rather arbitrary. The following are the contributions to gross domestic product for six of the years in the period under review, in constant factor costs and millions of Iraqi dinars, made by agriculture, fisheries, and forestry, the last two being negligible magnitudes:

1953	1954	1955	1956	1957	1958 [11]
86.59	114.80	69.43	89.23	117.76	90.47

The great variability of the yields makes it difficult to discern a trend: 1958 in comparison with 1953 shows a 5 percent gain in five years, while 1957 shows a gain of 36 percent in four years. The former relation means an average gain of 1 percent a year while population grew at 2.6 percent; the latter relation would imply gain of 9 percent a year. In view of the much greater importance of oil, these comparisons are not very significant. Furthermore, the investment in agriculture was primarily of a long-run character.

Industry

During the 1950–58 period, government policy for economic development was heavily oriented toward agriculture and toward industries based upon it. Doubtless the *persistence* in this direction was in part ascribable to reports by the International Bank (1952), Iversen (1954), and Salter (1955), all of which—as has been pointed out earlier—warned against excessive preoccupation with industry. That the recom-

---

[11] Central Bank of Iraq, *Annual Report 1963*, p. 153 (1956 prices).

mended course was a natural one, however, is shown by the activities of the Industrial Bank created by the government in 1940 to aid private industry, though its operations were always relatively modest compared to the oil revenues governed by the Development Board.[12] Both its participations in private industry by stock ownership and its loans were made preponderately in industries directly involved with agriculture or based upon a supply of raw materials from domestic agriculture.

In addition to direct financial aid, private industry received benefits from the Encouragement of Industry Law of 1950; new industries were granted exemption from certain taxes and the free use of government land for specified intervals; and industry enjoyed extensive tariff protection. Nevertheless, private industry in Iraq, as revealed by the Industrial Census of 1954, remained on a relatively primitive footing. In a country with a population of 8 million, industrial establishments aside from the petroleum industry employed only 90,291 laborers, of whom 45 percent worked in a one-man business and 93 percent were employed in firms of five or fewer persons. Industries based on agriculture accounted for 61 percent of employment and 61 percent of sales.[13]

During the typical year of the Industrial Census (1954) Iraq made substantial imports of consumers goods, chiefly in the categories of food, textiles, and durables. Dr. Langley poses the interesting question as to why Iraqi entrepreneurs did not try to displace these imports by products of local origin. Regarding one of the chief foods, sugar, the uncertainties of a new domestic product were deterrent; other imported foods were of a luxury variety with too small a domestic market. Durable consumer goods, such as stoves, air coolers, sewing machines, etc., required higher skills than the country possessed.

In line with the recommendations of the three reports by foreign agencies or economists, the Development Board directed its own industrial projects into fields in which the product depended upon domestic raw materials. The first Six Year Plan period witnessed the launching of a bitumen plant at Quaiyarah, a sugar beet refinery at Mosul, two cement plants, and a chemical plant in the Kirkuk area; it also supplied funds for an oil refinery in Daura, a village on the outskirts of Baghdad, oriented toward domestic consumption.

Early in the second Six Year Plan period (1956–60), the American firm of Arthur D. Little drew up an industrial plan for investing ID 43 million over the next six or seven years. It included a steel mill, paper manufacture, and industries designed to utilize Iraqi dates. But the most extensive part pertained to chemicals and petrochemicals: rayon, caustic soda, lime, ethylene, and sulphur from natural gas, plastics, and fertilizer. The Little report proved to be very influential, and many of the recommendations were immediately incorporated into the Plan. The sulphur recovery project had the double attraction of a valuable product and the removal of an element deleterious to the pipelines. At a later juncture, when Iraq turned to the USSR for capital, this was one of the chief projects to be activated.

---

[12] In 1956, for example, when the total loans and investment of the Industrial Bank amounted to ID 3,877,186, the expenditures of the board were (for fiscal 1956–57) ID 4 million.

[13] Langley, *op. cit.*, p. 89, *et seq.* Much of the substance of the present and next sections has been drawn from this excellent source.

35

Infrastructure and Social Overhead

In the category of industrial infrastructure, the Development Board made invest-ments of ID 4 million in the port of Basra and in the beginnings of a new port at Um Qasr. Highways were constructed, but the decade of the sixties did not witness the emergence of an adequate network of road transportation. ID 25 million was allocated in the 1955–60 Plan to improve the railway system, including conversion of the two-gauge system to a uniform width. The program included outlays on construc-tion and improvement of airports, including the facility at Baghdad. Finally, the Development Board undertook to utilize some of Iraq's extensive potential for the generation of electricity inherent in its oil and gas reserves and new impounding dams. Plants were under construction or being expanded at Dibis, Baghdad, and Basra. From 1950 to 1956, electric consumption rose from 116.8 to 506.3 million kilowatt hours.

In the field of education, the Ministry had expanded its annual outlay from ID 848 thousand (11.8 percent of the government budget) in 1940–41 to ID 3.6 million (14 percent) in 1950–51; and to ID 12.9 million (18.3 percent) in 1957–58. Attendance at primary schools rose by 10,000 per annum between 1945–46 and 1950–51, and by 42,000 in 1956–57. But the drop-out rate was high, so that much of the added literacy was virtually wasted. Furthermore, of the 1.5 to 2 million persons age 5 to 19, only one-fourth to one-third were to be found in the schools. Only slight progress had been made toward Iraq's goal of universal literacy. However, the Ministry of Education opened three commercial, three agricultural, and two technical high schools, expanded the facilities for the education of school teachers, launched the construction of a University of Baghdad, and considerably increased the number of Iraqi university students on government stipends abroad over its 1954 level of 3,000.

The Oil Industry

The conspicuous role of the oil industry in the economy of Iraq, in financing the government and supplying the wherewithal for economic development has been described. It accounts for a third or more of the national income; it is the largest single enterprise, but because little refining is done in Iraq, the industry ranks below the government as an employer. In this role, it has generally adopted the policy of paying wages slightly above the market level, acting as a sort of pacesetter. In matters of housing, training, recreation, medical treatment, and the like, its policies have been liberal. However, along with this paternalism, the industry was regarded as inimical to labor unions; at any rate no unions existed prior to the revolution of 1958.

Early in the decade of the fifties, the oil companies instituted a policy of "integra-tion," which meant widespread effort to become a part of the economy of Iraq. The policy has involved utilizing as extensively as possible domestic supplies and contrac-tors, hiring Iraqis in responsible positions, participating in civic and welfare projects, and pursuing liberal policies with respect to labor.

A Retrospect, 1950–58

To the economist interested in the general theme of economic development, this is a significant period for the light it sheds on the important issue as to what money alone can accomplish. What did the massive injections of income into the Iraqi economy beginning in 1950 do for the economy? Were the gains real or illusory; were they permanent or transitory? Did they benefit the common man?

In 1953 (the first year of national income accounting for the country) the net national product at factor cost (national income) was ID 262.82 million, and by 1958 it had risen in real terms (at 1956 prices) to ID 363.17 million.[14] Between these dates, the total increase of net national product (adding annual increases and subtracting decreases) amounted to ID 100.4 million. Proceeding the same way with oil production, we have a total increase of ID 46.6 million over the five years. Comparing one total increase with the other, we find the national income increase to be slightly over twice as large as the increase of oil production. If we attributed the whole increase of net national income to oil production, we could say that it has a multiplier effect of 2; but this would mean that no part of the increase would be attributed to other activities within the economy. Obviously this would clearly be a warrantable conclusion only if, over a series of years in which oil production did not increase, there were also no increase of national income. Since that evidence is not available, we are thrown back upon plausible inferences as to cause and effect.

The section on agriculture was not able to establish any clear trend of output from 1950 through 1958. Oil revenues devoted to flood control, irrigation, and drainage therefore had no clearly visible immediate effect, aside from the undoubtedly enormous psychological gain to the populace, both rural and urban, in immunity from floods from 1956 on, a gain which does not enter into the national income accounting. Aside from this, however, it would be difficult to deny that the Development Board made wise investments for agriculture, responsible for a third of national income, from a long-run angle.

With regard to manufacturing, including refining, its contribution to national income in 1958 at ID 36.54 million represented a rise of 83 percent since 1953. In construction, another field of great activity of the Development Board, either by direct investment or by indirect aid, the increase amounted to almost exactly 100 percent. Taken together, manufacturing and construction generated only about 13 percent of national income in 1953 but rose to 18 percent in 1958. Since agriculture did not register an increasing trend in the period, if the outlays of the Developing Board are to account for a substantial amount of non-oil income, we must look beyond agriculture and industry.

Examination of the details of net national income as recorded in the table on p. 38 shows dramatically that increases pervaded all categories. But since no item in the statistical picture amounts to more than a fraction of "crude oil extraction," one must conclude that this was the prime mover, directly through its own outlays in the economy, and indirectly in the effects of the expenditure of oil royalties going 30 percent to the general government budget and 70 percent to the Development Board. An increase of 38 percent in real national income over the five years 1953–58, or 7.6 percent per annum, is a very substantial advance.

However, the bare fact is that the period ended in a revolution. While public health and education showed improvements, and while the inadequate statistical evidence shows a virtual disappearance of unemployment and a rise of real wages,[15] the activi-

[14] See the table of Gross National Product of Iraq 1953–63, on p. 38.
[15] Qubain, *op. cit.*, p. 255.

Iraq: Gross Domestic Product, Gross National Product, and Net National Product at Constant (1956) Factor Cost Prices, 1953–63

(in millions of ID)

SECTOR	1953	1954	1955	1956	1957	1958	1959	1960	1961	1962	1963
1. Agriculture, forestry, and fishery											
(a) Field crops	30.81	44.36	21.03	28.45	42.46	28.50	19.69	22.07	28.01	34.89	16.83
(b) Vegetables	15.08	20.56	8.18	14.05	18.68	9.96	4.22	8.89	13.98	15.79	17.67
(c) Fruits and dates	7.73	9.65	7.38	6.73	9.17	8.16	4.05	5.38	7.89	9.50	6.03
(d) Livestock	31.25	38.37	30.91	37.59	44.95	41.22	37.12	38.63	45.82	52.56	38.42
(e) Forestry	0.96	1.02	1.06	1.12	1.18	1.27	1.29	1.19	1.21	0.93	1.00
(f) Fishery	0.76	0.84	0.87	1.29	1.32	1.36	1.39	1.42	1.46	1.49	1.54
Total agriculture, forestry, and fishery	86.59	114.80	69.43	89.23	117.76	90.47	67.76	77.58	98.37	115.16	81.49
2. Mining and quarrying											
(a) Crude oil extraction	128.91	149.53	161.16	152.45	107.34	175.47	203.90	235.50	244.10	246.08	280.93
(b) Other mining and quarrying	0.89	0.93	1.56	1.64	1.74	1.85	1.81	1.68	2.15	1.86	1.84
Total mining and quarrying	129.80	150.46	162.72	154.09	109.08	177.32	205.71	237.18	246.25	247.94	282.77
3. Manufacturing											
(a) Oil refining	1.91	2.46	3.45	4.19	4.99	6.00	6.72	8.08	9.60	9.89	10.15
(b) Other manufacturing	18.08	20.26	23.73	27.88	28.91	30.54	36.83	45.06	48.19	52.98	51.78
Total manufacturing	19.99	22.72	27.18	32.07	33.90	36.54	43.55	53.14	57.79	62.87	61.93
4. Construction	13.63	18.87	23.09	24.83	27.68	27.41	24.41	19.63	20.34	16.63	17.06
5. Electricity and water	1.33	1.43	2.13	2.53	2.99	3.18	3.45	4.12	5.43	6.44	6.64
6. Transport, communication, and storage	22.46	23.05	24.92	27.55	28.48	28.60	30.91	36.11	41.40	43.19	42.06
7. Wholesale and retail trade	19.16	23.73	22.60	26.90	29.02	26.69	24.59	30.08	36.00	38.15	33.43
8. Banking, insurance, and real estate	3.87	5.15	5.89	6.28	7.84	8.82	8.59	9.20	9.33	9.73	9.61
9. Ownership of dwellings	11.58	11.85	12.15	12.47	12.75	13.06	13.44	13.80	14.19	14.56	14.95
10. Public administration and defence	22.68	23.93	27.68	28.12	29.70	34.48	40.69	40.03	47.75	55.45	61.60
11. Services	20.58	22.12	23.31	24.83	25.57	27.45	30.87	35.03	41.99	43.56	45.15
12. Gross domestic product at factor cost	351.67	418.11	401.10	428.90	424.77	474.02	493.97	555.90	618.84	653.68	656.69
13. Less income to abroad	66.80	71.94	75.01	65.49	44.66	78.56	93.26	109.80	112.40	112.44	128.89
14. Gross national product at factor cost	284.87	346.17	326.09	363.41	380.11	395.46	400.71	446.10	506.44	541.24	527.80
15. Less provision for the consumption of fixed capital	22.05	23.54	27.12	28.65	31.71	32.29	32.11	33.42	37.81	38.11	38.34
16. Net national product at factor cost (national income)	262.82	322.63	298.97	334.76	348.40	363.17	368.60	412.68	468.63	503.13	489.46

Source: Dr. Khayr El Din Haseeb, in Central Bank of Iraq, *Annual Report 1963*, Baghdad, Iraq, 1964.

ties of the Development Board were not sufficiently successful in the short run to satisfy important sectors of the population. The board's expenditures on behalf of agriculture probably benefited the well-to-do strata of the countryside, and in the cities the housing program was too long delayed. Unfortunately a large role may have been played by what one Arab writer describes as a "philosophy of power" in foreign relations, which equated power with industrialization alone.[16]

Political Chaos in Iraq, 1958–69

The Kassem Regime, 1958–63

On July 14, 1958, a revolution under army leadership ended the monarchy in Iraq, instituting a military regime under General Kassem. So far as concerns economic factors underlying the overthrow of the kingdom, the failure of the oil revenue millions to trickle downward to any marked degree played an important role with the masses, and the decision of the Development Board to support long-run agricultural investments ran counter to the industry syndrome of many progressive intellectuals.[17] General Kassem, whose economic knowledge apparently bordered on nothing, promised great things to these disaffected extremes. He declared: "Three or four years from today the standard of the people will be great. . . . We will have heavy factories, and the farmer will be dignified and no one will remain without work."[18]

In 1958 a Land Reform Act limited individual ownership to 620 acres of irrigated or 1,240 acres of rain-fed land; at the same time an attempt, largely unsuccessful, was made to introduce cooperative farming. The land reform administration underwent three reorganizations in as many years. From a high point of output in 1957 at ID 117.8 million, agricultural output fell to ID 90.5 and ID 67.8 million (in constant prices) during 1958 and 1959. By June 1961, less than 10 percent of the nine million acres promised the peasants had been distributed.[19] By May 1963, about three-fourths of land subject to seizure had been "confiscated," but most of this had been re-leased by the Ministry of Agrarian Reform to the former owners as interim tenants! [20] While this was scarcely "agrarian reform," the former owners at least restored agricultural output, which reached its 1957 level again in 1962. But five years of potential growth were lost.

The Kassem regime drew up a Detailed Economic Plan for the period 1961–62 to 1965–66, to be financed partly by anticipated oil revenues and partly from domestic and foreign borrowing, involving expenditures totaling $1.5 billion. (Oil revenues from 1960 to 1962 were running at $265 million annually.) However, any substantial beginnings upon this somewhat fantastic plan proved impossible because the private sectors of the economy mistrusted the government and its relations with Egypt, and because the government was distracted and burdened by the guerrilla warfare waged by the Kurds. Gross national product at constant prices continued to rise during the years of the Kassem government, from ID 395.5 million in 1958 to ID 489.5 in 1963.

---

[16] Langley, *op. cit.* p. 267.

[17] Among noneconomic factors contributing to the revolt: isolation from the Arab world; too close ties to the West; repression.

[18] Quoted by Kathleen M. Langley, "Iraq: Some Aspects of the Economic Scene," *The Middle East Journal*, Spring 1964, p. 181.

[19] Don Peretz, *The Middle East Today* (New York: Holt, Rinehart, and Winston, Inc., 1963), p. 393.

[20] Langley, "*Iraq: Some Aspects . . . ,*" *op. cit.*, p. 186.

But national income at constant prices excluding oil revenues rose only by 26.8 percent over the six years, while oil revenue to the Iraqi government rose by 63.75 percent.[21] The increasing dependence of the economy upon oil revenue during the period is apparent. There can be no doubt that, in the words of Professor Lenczowski, "in the economic sector, Iraq under Kassem suffered a definite setback."[22]

Continued Political Turmoil after 1963

In February 1963, the "holy month of Ramadan," which gave its name to this revolution, the socialist Baath party displaced and executed General Kassem; it remained in the saddle only until November, when another coup replaced its rule with the military. On April 13, 1966, President Arif, two cabinet ministers, and seven aides were killed in a helicopter crash near Basrah; on June 30 an attempted coup against the new president (likewise named Arif) was crushed. But on July 17, 1968, a coup overthrew him in favor of a coalition of the Baath party and the military. The coalition in turn was superseded on July 31, 1968 by the Baath, the party which has remained in power to the present writing. Early in 1966 the government had approved an arrangement for the Arab Socialist Union to be the only legal party in the country; and on January 12, 1968, the students of Baghdad declared a strike because the government failed to provide for a parliamentary democracy. Interspersed among these events there were a number of more or less complete changes of cabinets, some of them reflecting the ebb and flow of political support for Nasser and alliance with the United Arab Republic.

In the midst of this political turbulence, it is small wonder that the course of economic development was frequently changed and interrupted. On June 2, 1964, it was announced that the "socialist measures" applied in the United Arab Republic would not necessarily be applied in Iraq under the proposed union between the two countries. A political union of this sort did not become a working reality, but the "socialist measures" were not long in abeyance. On July 14, 1964, the government announced the nationalization of the banks, insurance companies, and 32 industrial concerns, including all those producing asbestos, cement, cigarettes, textiles, paper, tanned leather, and flour. Two years later, on September 16, 1966, the Premier of Iraq announced that "the government has no further plans for nationalization"; but on December 3, 1967, all 16 of the privately owned newspapers were taken over by the government. Diplomatic relations with the United States, the United Kingdom, and West Germany were severed in 1967 because of their alleged espousal of the cause of Israel in the six-day June war. The interim constitution was extended in May 1968, for two years and general elections were postponed for the interval. The country had clearly joined the ranks of totalitarian socialist states. Statistical and other types of information regarding the economy became increasingly tardy and scarce.

A new economic Five Year Plan for the period 1965–66 to 1969–70 was put into effect. For a number of years previously, the main emphasis had been placed upon construction, transportation, communications, and industry. In the last category,

---

[21] Central Bank of Iraq, *Annual Report 1963*, p. 158.

[22] George Lenczowski, "Iraq: Seven Years of Revolution," *Current History*, May 1965, pp. 281–89; reprinted as No. 182, Middle Eastern Series. Institute of International Studies, University of California, Berkeley.

public sector projects had included sulfur extraction, textiles, paper, pharmaceuticals, and glass. The new plan gave greater importance to agriculture and contemplated investments as follows:

Public Investment Program, 1965-66–1969-70

(in millions of dollars)

	Estimated expenditures	Percent of total
Agriculture	$ 398	25%
Industry and electricity	440	28
Transportation and services	255	16
Government buildings and services	304	20
Other	174	11
Total	$1,571	100%
	Estimated resources	
Government savings	$1,134,000	
(50% of oil reserves)		
Domestic borrowing	171,000	
Foreign borrowing	266,000	
Total	$1,571,000	

Source: U.S. AID, *Economic Data Book, Near East and South Asia*, Iraq, p. 10. Revision No. 269, July 1968.

In 1964, the Export-Import Bank made long-term loans to Iraq aggregating $7.5 million, and in 1966 an additional $5 million for U.S. equipment for a generating plant in Baghdad, but the breaking of diplomatic relations in 1967 terminated U.S. aid. However, the International Bank made a loan in that year (which had been previously arranged) of $23 million for development projects. Soviet financial assistance was given for a dam on the Euphrates River at Haditha, for an atomic reactor, for drilling machinery, and engineering goods, amounting by mid-1967 to $84 million.[23] During the first two years of the last Five Year Plan, there was a reported short-fall of 43 percent in development finance caused by a diversion of oil revenues from economic development to ordinary budget. In 1968 oil revenues increased substantially, but internal development activity was reputed to be continuing at a low level.

In recent years, Iraqi economic history has not been prepossessing. Judged from the angle of the most general economic measures—gross national product in total and per capita—there has been a retrogression, reflected in the accompanying table. Aggregate GNP at current prices showed only a barely perceptible advance even in 1967, chiefly because of the setback to petroleum production in consequence of the Suez war and the Syrian stoppage of the flow of oil from Kirkuk to the Mediterranean. Put into real terms, GNP fell back in 1967 nearly to the 1963 level. Meanwhile popula-

[23] To the same juncture, the total U.S. economic assistance from 1946 on was $49.9 million and military assistance, $46.7 million, i.e., for both purposes, $96.6 million.

41

Iraq: Selected Annual Trends, 1964–68

Item	Unit	1964	1965	1966	1967	1968
GNP current prices [a]	Mill. dinars	702.6	742.9	798.2	800.0	n.a.
GNP 1963 prices	Mill. dinars	667.5	735.5	758.3	688	n.a.
GNP per capita deflated	Dinars	88.7	90.8	95.2	81.4	
Wholesale price index	1963 = 100	105	101	105	114	n.a.
Agri. production index	1957/58 = 100	105	108	104	107	120 [P]
Agri. prod. per capita	1957/58 = 100	86	86	81	81	88 [P]
Petroleum production	1,000 MT	61,627	64,473	68,004	60,168	73,848
Cement production	1,000 MT	1,092	1,285	1,210	1,193	10 months 1,002
Exports f.o.b.	Mill. U.S.$	840	882	939	828	10 months 867
Imports c.i.f.	Mill. U.S.$	−413	−451	−493	−423	10 months −343
Trade balance	Mill. U.S.$	425	431	446	405	10 months 524
Petroleum exports by volume [b]	1963 = 100	109	114	120	105	130
Government revenue [c]	Mill. dinars	209	225	214	261	293 [d]
from oil	Mill. dinars	129	136	123	152	163 [d]
from other sources	Mill. dinars	80	89	91	109	130 [d]
non-oil as % of oil	Percent	61.2	65.4	73.9	71.7	79.3 [d]
Government expenditure	Mill. dinars	256	245	243	277	375 [d]
on capital projects	Mill. dinars	59	61	49	52	145 [d]
capital as % of total	Percent	23.0	24.9	20.2	18.8	38.7 [d]
Government deficit	Mill. dinars	−47	−20	−29	−16	−82 [d]
deficit as % of expenditures	Percent	18.4	8.1	11.8	4.3	35.6 [d]

[c] = fiscal year; [d] = budget basis; [P] = provisional.

Sources: U.S. AID, *Economic Data Book, Near East and South Asia*, Iraq, p. 5, Revision No. 284, July 1969, except for [a] (1964, 1965) and [b] (all years) from International Monetary Fund, International Financial Statistics, November 1959, pp. 166, 169.

tion rose from 7 to 8.4 million. This fact, in conjunction with a rise of prices by 9 percent, reduced per capita real income in 1967 to ID 81.4, compared to ID 88.7 in 1964. If the disastrous year 1967 is omitted, per capita GNP *rose* by 3 percent per year from 1963 to 1966. But this is a considerable decline in the rate of economic development even from the preceding Kassem period (1958–63), which registered a 4.3 percent per annum increase of per capita GNP. It is a still greater fall from the years of the first Plan (1953–58) at 5.6 percent. National income figures for 1958 and 1959 are not available.

Because income accounting is particularly hazardous in Middle Eastern countries, this evidence requires supplementing by other indicators. Agriculture, which determines the income of half or more of the population, rose only by slightly less than 15 percent over the whole five years beginning in 1964, while per capita income scarcely advanced at all. Cement production, which is a fair gauge of industrial, bridge, utility, and water projects, maintained a constant level. Some improvement was shown in the first ten months of 1968 by foreign trade with a rise of exports and a decline of imports, producing an increased trade balance.

Turning finally to the sphere of public finance, we should note first that all numbers in the table for 1968 are budgetary figures, which express plans and intentions rather than accomplished facts. Many of these figures are out of line and must be taken *cum grano salis*. The decline of capital expenditures relative to others is a discouraging trend for the period. But two other relationships show improvement. Government revenue derived from other sources beside oil royalties rose relative to oil income, signifying—for this period at least—a diminished dependence on a wasting asset. Also, and again neglecting the budgetary figure in 1968, the fiscal deficit declined relative to government expenditures.

Iraq's Economic Position

Among Middle East countries, Iraq—with $362 million in oil income in 1967—occupied fourth place in the Middle East, with 43 percent of Saudi Arabia's and half of Iran's and Kuwait's oil revenues. In Iraq, this income plus the outlays of foreign oil companies have been associated in a rough way with a growth of GNP of twice this magnitude. Thus the multiplier effect of oil production seems to be great, since neither Iraqi production in agriculture, industry, nor indeed all domestic activities together can rival the petroleum industry. But oil wealth does not solve all problems: short-run variations of national income have not always been traceable to oil, and the 50-year reserves of petroleum in the earth cannot obliterate the fact that it is, after all, a wasting asset.

It is probably a general weakness of countries in the early phases of development to underrate the importance of cultural and institutional matters relative to physical factors such as oil, factories, and the like. Iraq illustrates this shortcoming in a number of ways. That oil revenue allocated to economic development was, for several initial years, expended only to 50 percent dramatizes the shortage of business and technical skills as bottlenecks of prime importance. In agriculture, purely physical matters such as irrigation, flood control, and drainage—however important in themselves—were allowed to eclipse almost completely the whole nexus of land tenure problems, agritural techniques, labor welfare and incentives, and the like. This too exclusive engineering approach, of which Doreen Warriner has complained with especial acerbity in the case of Iraq, was certainly a factor in the 1958 revolution. Revolutions and strife bordering upon revolution, costing Iraq a great deal in material terms in the past decade or so, are not technological matters, but social, economic, and political phenomena.

Thus a sad lesson from Iraq's recent history is the indispensability of domestic peace and tranquillity to economic development. Two centuries ago Adam Smith placed this first in the order of requirements for the growth of a nation's "annual produce." Domestic peace and tranquillity are not apt to be realized unless a part of the gains of economic development accrue to the broad masses.

Equally conspicuous in the case of Iraq is the lesson that military government is not necessarily wise and benevolent. The repute of army officers in the Middle East as the chief bearers of advanced ideas in the economic and social field—not without foundation in older regimes—has failed to justify itself more recently. Thus, for example, the regime of Abd al-Karim Kassem, by continuing policies of discrimination and neglect toward the Kurds, contributed to the outbreak of a civil war which long outlasted its tenure of government. "The allegedly socialist, progressive, nationalist officer regimes have only succeeded in plunging the Iraqi economy into such deep and prolonged crisis that development work has been at a near standstill over the past decade." [24]

---

[24] D. C. Watts, "Second Thoughts About the Military," *The New Middle East*, September 1969, pp. 36–37.

Against the present handicaps of the country are to be set not only its wealth in oil but also in the possibilities of petrochemical industries and diversified agriculture. Although the rate of population increase at 2.5 percent annually is disquieting, the low population density gives Iraq time in which to master its demographic problem. Meanwhile, the main economic problem is really political—the attainment of domestic stability. The annals of the past decade proclaim eloquently that, for genuine economic progress, oil is *not* enough.

III. MODERN TURKEY: AN EXPERIMENT IN STATE CAPITALISM

What Does Turkish State Capitalism Mean?

Seeking an appropriate label for the distinctive character of Turkish economic policy since the beginning of the Republic in 1923, most writers have called it "étatism." This connotes, of course, a large measure of state control over economic life; but simply to say "socialism" would be wide of the mark. "State socialism," borrowing a term often used for the policies of Bismarck in the 1870s in Germany, might be fair enough; but "state capitalism" would be even better. What are the distinctive features of the Turkish variant of socialism?

For one thing, there has been no fixed ideological basis, as for example Marxism; "Turkish étatism," says one historian, "was not really true to any principle." Nor was there any overtone of the internationalism of a classical but virtually nonexistent socialism. More distinctive is the fact that the government, while absorbing a large fraction—perhaps 40 percent—of the nation's industrial base, did not aim at making the state the exclusive economic agent. Agriculture—which now accounts for 35 percent of the national product, 75 percent of employment, and up to 90 percent of exports—remains private; important industries were never nationalized; and significant steps were taken to encourage private enterprise. State activity was resorted to only when private undertakings proved inadequate, but some fields were taken over for strategic or political reasons.

These are the basic characteristics of étatism or state socialism as defined in 1933 by the Republican People's party, the party of Ataturk, founder of the Republic.[1] In subsequent years a bitter conflict arose within the CHP (Republican People's party) between the moderates, who continued to support the founders' views, and the extremists, who rejected the ideal of a mixed economy, in which public and private sectors live in harmony. Nationalization would progress inexorably with no returning of particular sectors to private auspices. In the course of time a middle-of-the-road position developed, still retaining the strong impress of the original party declaration, which holds to this day.

---

[1] Memduh Yasa, "Marshalling of Capital by the State and Direct Investment in Industry: Turkish Experience," in *Capital Formation and Investment in Industry* (Istanbul: Economic and Social Studies Conference Board, 1963), pp. 94–99.

Marked by these differences between the Turkish form and the socialism or communism of the USSR and its satellites, etatism was an integral part of the policy of Mustafa Kemel (Ataturk), the founder of the Republic. It imbued but did not dominate three developmental plans from the first (1934–39), through the second (1937–42) and the third (1946–50), and on down to the contemporary scene. This is true despite the "revolution" of 1950 with the advent of the Democratic party, which promised a liberal regime in the Manchesterian sense, but which in fact did not affect the prevailing etatism. In 1960 and again in 1964, the Republican People's party returned to power, representing a remarkable degree of political continuity and stability by Middle East standards.

What forces impelled the Turkish Republic into the state socialist or state capitalist mould? A leading Western historian lays it partly to "the ambition of empire-building bureaucrats" on the one hand, and, on the other hand, to the scarcity of private capital and to the failure of private enterprise to achieve the desired pace of development. No doubt the strongly military, authoritarian traditions of the Ottoman Empire played a role. The apparent triumphs celebrated by Fascist Italy, Nazi Germany, and Soviet Russia in the thirties impressed the young Turkish Republic at a formative stage. Finally, etatism was partly the result of the first world war, when native capitalists were unable or unwilling to take over the enterprises being vacated by foreign owners; the state filled the vacuum.[2]

In a brief span we have indicated the complexion of the economic regime prevailing in Turkey—the most populous country of the Middle East—during the near half century which has elapsed since the foundation of the Republic. What does the record show about its performance? In 1960, the government was able to point to a rise of literacy from 10.6 percent in 1923 to 40.1 percent, to an increase of the total number of students by tenfold, to a rise in the number of hospital beds by fifteenfold, a doubling of the railway network, and a trebling of the total length of highways and great improvement in their quality.

On the other hand, the government candidly confessed that: "Great masses live in very primitive conditions without any of the benefits of civilization. 60 percent of the population of school age and above are illiterate. 53 percent of the villages and 55 percent of the small towns have either no, or inadequate, drinking water. . . . There is only one doctor to every 4,000 inhabitants. 30 percent of city dwellings are unfit for habitation."[3]

Subsequent pages will attempt to account for the simultaneous existence of outstanding accomplishments and equally conspicuous shortcomings of Turkish development, traced through successive phases of its history. But it is immediately evident that elements of an explanation of this paradox are to be found in some economic "facts of life" which distinguish the Turkish economy.

For one thing, the noteworthy advances, such as those illustrated above, are partly ascribable to the low ebb of the country after the first world war, which did not end for Turkey until 1922, four years after the armistice in Western Europe, piled upon three additional years of belligerency before 1914. Small wonder that domestic pro-

---

[2] Private capital was largely in the hands of minorities, who hesitated to invest after the special privileges (the "Capitulations") in the old regime were abolished by the Republic.

[3] Republic of Turkey, State Planning Organization, *First Five-Year Development Plan, 1963–1967* (Ankara: Central Bank of the Republic, 1964), pp. 1, 2, 8.

duction and foreign trade were so disrupted that the index of per capita national income stood in 1922 at 53 compared even with 1938 ($=100$) in the impoverished thirties. Thus, with so low a basis of comparison in the initial years of the Republic, its subsequent achievements are bound to seem large.

Another fact, however, is more important: the outstanding gains have been of an aggregative nature, expressible in such terms as GNP, miles of railway track and highways, and the like, whereas the shortcomings have pertained to the individual citizen and to the distribution of income and amenities. First and foremost, while GNP finally registered quite satisfactory rates of increase, the welfare gain was at times canceled out and at other times greatly diluted by the increase of population.

A kindred factor relates to the relatively favorable endowment of Turkey in natural resources, aside of course from the incredible wealth of some of its neighbors in oil. Thus agricultural land, though not as abundant as in France, the United States, or New Zealand, is relatively plentiful in comparison with most countries of the Middle East. It is the backbone of the Turkish economy, and—as we shall see—proves to be the chief source of its growth. But the unequal distribution of land holding has retarded the improvement of the material lot of the vast mass of village and rural population. The gulf between town and country was profound in all respects. The urban minority had almost a monopoly on post-primary education. Surplus labor has been found chiefly in agriculture. "Doctors tend to concentrate in cities: in 1953 there were roughly twenty times more doctors per thousand of population in the province of Istanbul than in Van."[4] While agriculture supplies the larger part of Turkish national income and exports, the yearly output per rural earner, as calculated by Colin Clark in 1951, amounted to 119 international units, compared to 165 even in Syria, to say nothing of 414 units in France. Unfortunately, it is not the aggregate output of agriculture which determines the worker's income, but per capita productivity.

Similar reflections pertain to coal and iron, in which Turkey has a favorable resource base, enabling it alone in the Middle East to develop heavy industry of any size. International comparison revealed an output of iron per worker per shift of .47 tons in Turkey as against 1.15 in Great Britain and 4.37 in the United States. In industry as a whole for the same countries, outputs measured in international units were, respectively, 345, 870, and 1,849. However industry may have fared in Turkish development, its significance for the individual worker has not been impressive. Many historical and cultural factors are responsible for this circumstance, but the share of blame to be borne by government in general and by the halting pace of labor legislation in particular is not large. In the present context, its relevance is that there are "many a slip" between substantial advances in national aggregates and gains in individual welfare. Obviously government saving and investment may, as in the Turkish case, represent another important deflection.

The present preview of the record of economic development in Turkey is not concerned solely with the contrasting behavior of GNP magnitudes and welfare. There are certain economic facts in the Turkish case which have been important for both the aggregative and welfare aspects.

Referring again to natural resources, on the favorable side are the large output

---

[4] Royal Institute of International Affairs, *op. cit.*, p. 506.

and immense reserves of coal and iron, and the occurrence of chrome, a very lucrative export in the fifties, and copper, a more important export now. Agricultural land has been abundant in the sense that expansion of cultivated acreage has contributed strongly to the increase of national income, although the incursion of cultivation on pasturage is beginning to be felt in animal husbandry. An unfavorable element in nature is the great variability of rainfall and its effects upon dry-land wheat farming. Rivers running eastward in the province of Anatolia are said to offer possibilities for hydroelectric generation.

Man himself is, however, the chief determinant of his economic fate. As a "political animal," his behavior in one respect has been favorable to development: for 37 years— from the creation of the Republic in 1923 to the temporary take-over by the military in 1960—there was no forcible overthrow of any Turkish government and virtually no domestic turbulence, a record almost unique in the Middle East.[5] In another sense, domestic stability in the form of the unprogressive peasant and the large landholder with merely vestigial civic conscience has balked the taxation of agricultural income and the effective combating of inflation.

Foreign observers generally agree upon the prevalence in Turkey of certain attitudes inimical to economic development—hostility to cultural change, lack of respect for work, fatalism, paucity of scientific ways of thinking, etc. Traditionally the preferred careers for the upper middle class were military, civil service, or professional; when, reluctantly, it turned to business, it went into trade, finance, and brokerage, leaving industry to the concern of government. But after 1923, the civil service declined in popularity, while private entrepreneurship and other independent professions gained in prestige.

Periods of Recent Economic History

The history of Turkish efforts at economic development from the time of Ataturk to the present falls into five periods which almost define themselves through major events. The *Interwar Period* extends from 1923–38 and includes the first Five Year Plan. The second period, the *War Years* 1938–45, embraces the second Plan, 1937–42, which was terminated by the war. During the years 1945–50, the *Postwar Period*, the Turkish economy had to undergo reorientation and recovery. Beginning in 1950, a combination of circumstances brought about rapid growth despite the absence of a plan. This decade is the fourth period, *Inflationary Expansion*, 1950–60. Toward the end of the period internal strains developed, resulting in a take-over by the military in 1960. The fifth period, designated merely as the *Sixties*, after an initial interlude of transition, witnessed the introduction of the so-called first Five Year Development Plan, 1963–67, and the second Plan ensuing upon it.

The labels attached to these periods follow closely but not exactly those employed in the Turkish government's document bearing the name of the 1963–67 Plan. They are chosen to reflect the fact that the five-year plans have not really dominated the successive epochs. The Turkish economy is—after all—mixed; it is not the monolithic communism of the USSR. Within the broad category of mixed economies it lies somewhere between the models of, say, Norway and Yugoslavia.

---

[5] Except for the Kurdish rebellions, which in 1924–25 involved large units of the Turkish army. But even such uprisings disappeared after 1938.

The Interwar Years

The Ataturk revolution led to the proclamation of the Turkish Republic on October 29, 1923; and it was the ideas and drive of Mustafa Kemel which set Turkey on the path of state capitalism, enduring to the present. But this policy did not spring into being instantly, and the twenties were marked by relatively liberal measures. Thus the agricultural tax, a "symbol of the oriental feudal system" was abolished in 1925; a land tenure code based on the Swiss model was introduced; and private agriculture was aided by credit, agricultural schools, and cooperative stores. In 1927, a law for the encouragement of private industry exempted approved industries from certain taxes, granted a 30 percent reduction on rail and sea transport rates, and extended subsidies equalling 10 percent of the value of finished product.

However, a strong tendency also developed in the opposite direction. Among other steps was the establishment of specialized banks, operating with government capital, which were destined to become among the chief vehicles of state control of industry. Grunwald and Ronall call the founding of the Bank for Industry and Mines in 1925 "Turkey's first step in étatism." [6] But the Agricultural Bank had been founded in the nineteenth century with state capital. Later the Bank for Industry and Mines was supplanted by the Sümer Bank (1931), which became the central instrument of Turkish industrialization. The new Central Bank of Turkey (1931) and the Eti Bank for mineral resources and electric power continued this evolution.

The Labor Law of 1936, resting on a 1933 amendment to the Penal Code prohibiting strikes and lockouts, delivered employer-employee relations completely into the hands of the state. Finally, in the early years of the Republic, the government became the owner of monopolies in salt, sugar, matches, alcoholic beverages, tobacco, and explosives, as well as the conventionally nationalized services such as railroads, maritime passenger and air transportation, and the postal service.

Thus, during the first decade after 1924 state capitalism or state socialism had taken root in the soil of Turkey. But it was the depression of the thirties, an apparent failure of the free enterprise system in Europe and America, coupled with the apparent success of the first Russian Five Year Plan, which gave the decisive thrust toward the Five Year Plan of 1934-39. Turkey became the first among the underdeveloped countries to conduct an experiment in planning.

Devised by the American consulting firm Hines, the program did not involve complete planning but aimed toward developing industries which would utilize raw materials found in the country, disperse industrial activity, alleviate rural unemployment, and encourage the textile and other consumers' goods industries. Not much was undertaken on behalf of agriculture; indeed this was the subject of adverse criticism. But national income rose in terms of 1938 prices from TL 1,315 million in 1935 to TL 1,652 million in 1939; despite an increase of population from 16.2 to 17.5 million, per capita real income rose from TL 82 to TL 95. Although agriculture was not emphasized by the first Five Year Plan, the value of its output grew by 20 percent in the decade of the thirties. Industry, however, registered the greatest gains. The great iron and steel mill at Karabük (later to reveal shortcomings) was built, and new enterprises were launched in paper, cement, textiles, glass, coal, aluminum, and copper. The

---

[6] Grunwald and Ronall, *op. cit.*, p. 331.

49

index of mineral production including coal, lignite, and chromium, rose in the decade 1930–40 from 100 to 232; and sugar, an industry utilizing domestic raw materials, increased its output by approximately twentyfold. In short, the plan realized most of its objectives, and the formulation of a new program was initiated well before 1939.

The War Years, 1939–45

Turkey assumed a nonbelligerent position in the second world war but suffered economically from the costs of mobilizing the army and from the severance of foreign trade. The second Five Year Plan set high targets for plant construction, rationalizing coal production, and building up of the engineering industry; but the outbreak of war put an end to implementing the plan. Over the war years, the price level rose by fourfold, while per capita real GNP rose over the whole seven-year period only at an average annual rate of 1 percent.

Postwar Years, 1946–50

Likewise, the period immediately after the war, ending in 1950 with the domestic political upheaval when the Democratic party succeeded the Republican government, was not an era of notable economic growth. A *Third Five Year Plan* was indeed announced in 1946 for chemicals, textiles, cement, wood pulp, paper, and iron and steel products, with increased emphasis on agriculture. But the plan proved largely abortive, because of the continuance of heavy military expenditures prompted by the country's understandable fears for its territorial integrity; because of the expectation of large foreign aid which did eventuate by the end of fiscal 1949/50 in $180 million of United States Marshall aid; and finally, because reserves of gold and foreign exchange accumulated by Turkey during the war had lost much of their efficacy for development through the limited supplies and high prices of importable investment goods. The etatist regime of Turkey was severely criticized by foreign experts in the American aid organization (ECA), the International Bank and the Thornburg group, for fostering monopoly and high costs of production.

The charge of monopoly might have been countered by the frank avowal that Turkey had espoused state capitalism. By 1948, in addition to the monopolies which have already been noted, the government owned entirely: coal mining, cellulose, paper, chemicals, iron, and steel; it owned virtually all of the power generating and broadcasting facilities, oil reserves and oil wells, and forests; glass manufacture and construction; 70 percent of chrome and lignite production and 65 percent of the merchant marine.

Nevertheless, since 1929 commerce and industry had increased only from 13 to 15 percent of national income; and the index of per capita income in real terms had risen only from 87 to 107 over the same period. But there were some noteworthy advances, such as the expansion of cultivated land from 13.8 to 17.3 percent of the total land area between 1934 and 1949, large increases in the capital of all the state banks, and a rapid doubling of the number of tractors with Marshall aid funds.

When the first popular election in Turkey was held in 1950, the Republican party, which had been in power for 27 years and which stood on a platform of government ownership and regulation, was swept out of office by the Democratic party, favoring a minimum of state control. In any event, the party was unable even to move toward this objective.

Inflationary Expansion, 1950–60

During the decade of the fifties, annual growth rates of per capita GNP describe a very high level through 1955 (sharply broken in 1954 by one negative value), and thereafter a continuous decline to a minus quantity in 1961, as shown in the accompanying table.

Turkey: Per Capita GNP in 1967 Prices, 1950–61

	1950	1951	1952	1953	1954	1955
Amount in U.S. dollars	202	226	238	258	229	239
Annual percent increase		12.4	5.3	8.6	−11.4	4.4

	1956	1957	1958	1959	1960	1961
Amount in U.S. dollars	249	257	262	265	268	256
Annual percent increase	4.2	3.2	1.9	1.1	1.1	−4.4

Source: U.S. Agency for International Development, *Gross National Product: Growth Rates and Trend Data by Region and Country*, April 25, 1969.

During the first eight years of the fifties, Turkey experienced continuous inflation, first of a mild sort from 1950 through 1953, and subsequently, from 1954 to the crisis of 1958, of the galloping variety. But the great boom of the eight-year period was more than monetary, as witnessed by the fact that the figures in the foregoing table have all been reduced to real terms by deflating to 1967 prices; they still show remarkable increases. In fact, the roots of the boom lay in real factors: the high conjuncture in the international economy caused by the Korean war, and the prosperity of Turkish agriculture resting on favorable weather conditions, fast mechanization and its attendant, a rapid expansion of cultivated acreage.[7]

Other indicators beside real GNP per capita show that the first part of the fifties was a period of genuine growth and prosperity. Thus, on the basis of 1948 = 100, output indices in 1956 stood as follows: power, 226.6; minerals, 186.5; manufacturing, 167.6; food, 208.3; and general production, 195.6. In addition, at the earlier and later dates, there were 21,334 and 28,717 kilometers of graded and surfaced roads; 10,596 and 34,429 trucks; and 10,000 and 41,000 tractors reaching 54,668 by 1965. There may be warrant for the rather categoric pronouncement that "no country had ever moved forward so fast."[8]

Unfortunately, the entire decade witnessed inflation, strong budgetary and balance-of-payments deficits, and their unwelcome accompaniments. Through 1953 the rise of prices was moderate, though the increases of money were certainly laying the ground

[7] I am indebted at this point, and at numerous others, to Professor Memduh Yasa of the University of Istanbul.

[8] Richard D. Robinson, *The First Turkish Republic, A Case Study in National Development* (Cambridge: Harvard University Press, 1965), pp. 148–52. The present chapter has drawn frequently on this excellent work.

51

Price Indices in Turkey, 1950–59 (1948 = 100)

Year	Wholesale prices	Retail prices in Istanbul
1950	96	105
1951	109	104
1952	107	111
1953	109	118
1954	119	135
1955	134	147
1956	157	169
1957	183	181
1958	223	215
1959	268	255

Source: First Chamber of Commerce and Conjuncture Section, Ministry of Commerce.

for a later outburst of price increases; from 1951 to 1952, bank deposits increased by 30 percent in the single year, and in 1953 by 31 percent. Much of this inflation in these years has been attributed to an expansion of Central Bank credit to finance the unsound accumulation of cereals by a government agency, the Soils Products Office.[9]

Price increases of ever-mounting size from year to year persisted through the balance of the decade, supported by expansion of the means of payment at a rate reaching a maximum in 1957. It is impossible to justify this behavior of the monetary authorities on the basis of a desire to stimulate the rate of investment for development purposes, since it declined steadily as a percentage of GNP from 1954 through 1958. The chief origins of Central Bank credits during this runaway stage were the losses incurred by state enterprises operating under price maxima, price maintenance on official purchases of grains, and concealed subsidies on exports, including those of the state monopoly of tobacco. In the last analysis, the cause underlying all of this was that "stopping the inflation and stabilizing the economy were considered disastrous from the political standpoint."[10]

The enormous budget deficit developing during the first half of the decade came to be covered by 1955 to 3/7 by external grants, 3/7 by money creation and the use of counterpart funds, and 1/7 by domestic and foreign borrowing. In consequence of these inflationary phenomena, the foreign trade deficit mounted from $22.3 to $184.3 million; Turkey became one of the largest debtors in the European Payments Union, with an outstanding amount of $297.3 million in 1954 and an annual service of $26.5 million. It seems warranted to conclude with R. D. Robinson that "the Turkish leaders adopted a policy of importing everything possible, worrying about payment later."

By 1955, economic developments, including a 15 percent rise in the cost of living in one year, brought the government into popular disfavor. In September there were riots in Istanbul and Izmir and the Prime Minister, Mederes, formed a new government, promising to promote private enterprise, balanced budgets, and monetary stability.

---

[9] This is the judgment of Osman Okyar in an excellent analysis "Inflation in a Mixed Economy," in Conference Board, op. cit., pp. 352–70.

[10] Okyar, op. cit., p. 366.

In December, price profit controls were decreed and ceilings were imposed on bank credits. Black market rates on the lira had risen to 8–10 to the dollar compared to the official rate of 2.8, leading to a tardy recognition of overvaluation in the special exchange rates of 1956 and 1958 on certain categories of exports and capital transactions. In the course of 1955, bilateral agreements were struck with Great Britain, Belgium, and Germany for the liquidation of clearing debts.

Out of these measures of attempted stabilization came the almost inevitable aftermath: retarded advance, which approached stagnation during the years 1959 through 1961, a year which actually registered a shrinkage of GNP. As often observed, it is difficult or impossible to break a strong inflationary movement without at least mild recession.

Looking back over the decade of the fifties, however, Turkey had reason to feel some satisfaction. Per capita real income had risen by 30 percent or an average of 3 percent per annum, despite a population increase of 28.7 percent or 2.87 per annum. Gross investments increased from 9.6 to 15.9 percent of GNP, despite national defense expenditures varying between 5.5 and 3.5 percent of GNP.[11] On the more human side also, the number of students approximately doubled, hospital beds increased from 18,800 to 45,000, and literacy improved from 33.6 to 40.1 percent.

The Decade of the Sixties

The measures adopted in the stabilization program of August 4, 1958, organized by the IMF resulted in an abatement of inflation, but the revolution of May 27, 1960, bringing the military into power, occurred before the full results could appear. In 1961 a State Planning Office was established, and in 1963 the first really full-fledged Development Plan went into effect. It was conceived as a part of a 15-year program aimed toward five main objectives: (1) an annual increase of GNP by 7 percent; (2) reduction of unemployment; (3) eventually refusing to accept foreign aid; (4) universal primary education; and (5) lessening of income inequalities. For the five years 1963–67, growth rates were projected for GNP at 7 percent, agriculture at 4.7 percent, and industry at 12.3 percent. In fact, these aims were very nearly realized: GNP with 6.6, agriculture with 3, and industry with 9.1 percent increases.

Over the five years of the plan period, production rose for certain products as follows in percent increases: cement, 82; tobacco, 76; wheat, 14; crude petroleum, nearly 50 from a small base; and electric power, 50. In addition the dollar f.o.b. value of exports increased by 34 percent. The behavior of specific sectors is reviewed in the following sections. It is worth pointing out in looking at the general record of the sixties, first, that the increases of aggregates and particular components of GNP were accomplished only with significant increases of prices and the cost of living. Secondly, that, despite the increase of exports, the balance of payments was strongly negative throughout; that the increase of imports was accompanied by heavy domestic investment, largely financed by foreign borrowing; and that this was not necessarily a mistaken course.

At the termination of the first full Development Plan in 1967, a second Five Year Development Plan was set afoot. The growth of GNP is aimed at 7 percent per annum,

---

[11] National defense forms a part of total investments, but the share fell over the decade from 44.2 to 29.7 percent.

a conservative goal in view of the 6 percent achieved under the first Plan. Considerable emphasis is laid upon expanding educational facilities, but the largest spheres of investment are to be manufacturing, TL 25 billion; housing, TL 20 billion; communications, TL 18 billion; and agriculture, TL 16.9 billion. Agriculture is to decline from 30.4 to 26.6 percent of GNP over the years 1967–72, industry rising from 25.2 to 30.7 percent. Attention is given to the problem of unemployment. Foreign aid should cease by or during the third Plan period, a goal thought to be realizable by Guenther Keiser, the president of the International Consortium for Aid to Turkey.

During 1968, the first year of the plan quinquennium, agriculture, always subject to fluctuations, showed a 1.1 percent increase in output, compared to 11.4 percent in 1966 and 0.9 in 1967, while industry actually declined from a 12.3 rate of increase in 1967 to 10.3 in 1968. Strong increases in rates were, however, registered in commerce and transportation; the net outcome was an increase of GNP at 6.6 percent, compared with 6.1 in 1967, auguring well so far as this large aggregate goes. Foreign indebtedness, however, increased by 11.3 percent; but the government deficit declined with an increase in the yield of direct taxes by 13.3 percent (March–November 1968), a most salutary development.

Development of the Economic Sectors

Agriculture

The share of agriculture in Turkish national income has always been large; it fell to a somewhat lower proportion during the thirties; but since then, while variable because of crop fluctuations, its level has not changed greatly. But the index of agricultural output, under the influence of strong help from the government, increased substantially, aside from the 1948 value which reflects wartime vicissitudes.

Agricultural Output in Turkey

	1927	1938	1948	1950	1958	1961	1966	1967	1968
Percent of national income	67	48	53	52	44	42	36.8	30.2	28.9
Index of output 1938 = 100	57	100	74	116	119	205	253	255	281

Source: *First Five Year Development Plan; Second Five Year Development Plan;* U.S. AID, *Economic Data Book, Near East and South Asia;* and *Turkish Economic Review,* March–April 1969.

Aid to agriculture was extended through tax abatements and price supports, though benefits also accrued in other ways. In the twenties, a traditional tax on the revenue of land called the Ösür was eliminated, plants and seeds were distributed gratis, and some state land was given to landless peasants. The thirties witnessed the institution of crop subsidy through minimum prices; at a time when the New York price of wheat was $1.50 a bushel, it was costing $2.21 to produce in Turkey. In 1945, all taxes on agricultural produce were eliminated. Especially in 1952 and 1953 the budgetary load occasioned by Toprak, the government price-support organization, contributed heavily to budgetary and balance-of-payments deficits. Just at the time of some of

54

the largest foreign deficits, agricultural credit expanded most rapidly. In the four years from 1949 to 1953, farm credit rose from TL 336.9 million to TL 1,172 million, or more than threefold. In addition to using its own resources preponderately for agriculture, Turkey applied a large fraction of American aid, amounting to $396.6 million over the critical years 1948–55, to farm machinery, of which tractors were the chief item. Over these years their number advanced from 1,746 to 41,000, reaching 54,688 by 1965.

Whether or not the favoring of agriculture in taxes, price supports, and farm credit has paid off is a disputed question. One trouble has been the short-run instability of returns; it has been pointed out that Turkey passed from being the world's fourth largest exporter of grain in 1953 to a net importer in 1955. The $2\frac{1}{2}$ fold increase of agricultural output noted above was not achieved by an increase of labor efficiency or superior farming techniques, but almost solely by extending the area cultivated by means of mechanization.

In defense of government policy, it may be said that it exploited the most abundant and readily available resource through four decades of development; now that the pushing of cultivation into new land cuts into animal husbandry severely, it is prepared to turn to other channels. The First Development Plan witnessed a decline of the agricultural share of production from 42 to 30.2 percent from 1961 to 1967; and the Second Plan contemplates a further reduction to 26.6 percent by 1972. In the future, the contribution of agriculture to the balance of trade could be strengthened by a growth of cotton and tobacco exports and diversification through fresh vegetables, fresh and dried fruits, nuts, forestry products, and meat.

A word is in order concerning land reform. The Turkish government has, of course, instituted other measures on behalf of the rural population, in the improvement of highways, health, credit, and education. But land reform in the sense of a redistribution of land has not progressed far. Laws providing for state distributions of land to impoverished peasants were passed in 1927, 1929, 1934, and 1937, but the amounts allocated were meager. In 1945 a rather pretentious law envisaged gifts of state land and the redistribution of private landed property over 1,250 acres. In fact no private land has been touched, and by the beginning of the sixties 23,310 square kilometers of state land, mostly of the dry-land-farming variety, had been given to 313,000 families (three million were engaged in agriculture!), an average of 18 acres per family. In 1961 and 1962 the statistical record shows an attenuation of grants to the vanishing point, and there is no evidence of a revival of activity subsequently.[12]

The extreme poverty of the bare-subsistence peasants can be at least faintly indicated by statistics. Some 308,000 families engaged in farming in 1963 possessed no land; in addition, 1.2 million farmers worked plots not exceeding 2,000 square meters, or about half an acre. Thus, of the total agricultural population of 3.1 million families, some 1.3 million were either landless or possessed of inadequate acreage. Even those owning up to 5,000 square meters, or $1\frac{1}{4}$ acres, constituting 68.8 percent of the total farming population, derived an average annual income per farm (family) unit of TL 2,900 (TL 9 = U.S. $1) at a time when TL 12,000 was estimated to be the minimum for a decent subsistence for an urban worker. At the opposite extreme, 3.57 percent of

---

[12] This account follows Z. Y. Herschlag's new opus, *Turkey: the Challenge of Growth* (Leiden: E. J. Brill, 1968), *passim*.

the farm units owned up to 100,000 square meters, or about 25 acres, with an average annual income per unit of TL 44,510, or enough to support the families of nearly four urban workers.

However, the amount of agricultural income accruing to owners of 100,000 square meters or more does not exceed 10 percent of the total; consequently, a redistribution of acreage from rich to poor would not do much toward alleviating rural poverty. The central problem is simply that the average size of farms is below the economically optimum size. The fragmentation of land caused by population increase and practices of inheritance frustrates efforts toward improved rural health, welfare, and morale. Beyond that, the small farms waste time and energy, foster disputes over boundaries, and depress the level of agricultural efficiency and output.[13]

Basically, therefore, *ad hoc* measures, such as land redistribution and welfare measures directed toward the rural population, while remedial, are not enough. The problem merges with the general problem of raising per capita income and reducing unemployment in the country as a whole. In this general context, attention should be directed toward elimination of uneconomic crops, such as sugar, supported by subsidies, toward better credit facilities for agriculture and toward returning marginal land to forests.

Industry

Industrial activity has grown and spread to new branches in Republican Turkey, but has played a much smaller role than agriculture. The increase of industry by four-

Industrial Output in Turkey

	1927	1938	1948	1950	1958	1961	1966	1967	1968
Percent of national income [1]	10	16	14	16	22	23	23	25.5	n.a.
Index of output [2] 1948=100	—	63	100	109	189	—	206	231	255

Source: for [1], Republic of Turkey, *First Five Year Development Plan*, p. 9; U.S. AID, *Economic Data Book, Near East and South Asia*, NESA Regional, Table 5, p. 11. Revision No. 273, September 1968; for 1967, computed from *Turkish Economic Review*, March–April 1969, p. 26; for [2], Herschlag, *Turkey, An Economy in Transition* (The Hague, Holland: van Keulen, n.d.), p. 235; values for 1967 and 1968, *Turkish Economic Review, loc. cit.*

fold greatly exceeded the 181 percent growth of agricultural output over the years 1938–66 and thus increased its share in national income by half, while agriculture fell. Some 40 percent of industry is in the hands of the state. The private sector has been stimulated by credits from the banking system, including the specialized government banks referred to earlier and the Industrial Development Bank, established with IBRD aid, and by foreign private investment, mainly American, German, and Italian. Furthermore, the development of the industrial infrastructure has been significant: a doubling of railroad mileage and a trebling of highways from 1923–60, and a twelvefold expansion of electric power output, 1940–65.

---

[13] "Turkish Agriculture Today," *Turkish Economic Review*, March–April 1968, pp. 43–47.

Since 88 percent of electric generating capacity is thermal, the expansion of power owes much to the exploitation of the vast reserves of coal, estimated at 1.3 billion tons of the Eregli-Zonguldak basin, with an annual output exceeding 5 million tons in 1967. Similarly the fortunate occurrence of both coal and iron deposits gives Turkey a unique position in heavy industry.

In 1936, construction was begun in the great steel and iron complex (blast furnaces, coke ovens, sintering plants) at Karabük. Its location was said to be unduly influenced by the iron ore deposits of the northwest compared to eastern Anatolia,[14] and the pig iron output exceeded the capacity of the steel mill. But these errors were partly absorbed by the growth process; in 1958 extensions engineered by the Krupp firm expanded the steel and iron capacity to 350,000 tons a year. Foreign aid has contributed to the financing of a second steel mill at Eregli.

It deserves, however, to be said that the total investment in the basic metals industry at TL 2.1 billion is exceeded by chemicals at TL 2.7 billion; that textiles are the largest employer of labor; and that in good crop years wheat is the most valuable export.

Turkey's industrialization, particularly in the first half of the decade of the fifties, when it was attended by inflation and unconscionable increases in foreign deficits and debts, has been criticized as exaggerated. Both the public and private sectors of industry, as the United States AID has pointed out, are characterized by high costs arising from high protective tariffs, careless labor, inexperienced management, small-scale production, and other factors. All of these are remediable ailments, however, which can be outgrown. That Turkish industry should increase seems clear, and whether its growth rate should or should not exceed that of agriculture is probably a less important problem than, say, the rate of population increase.

Welfare

From significant angles the Turkish citizen enjoys a level of economic welfare as high as—and sometimes higher than—his Middle Eastern neighbors. Thus the average level of caloric intake at 3,110 units per diem is not rivaled elsewhere in the region; malaria can now be regarded as under control; literacy, once at the very low level of 10.6 percent in 1927, was raised to 47 percent by 1968. The rate of population increase at 2.4 percent represents something like an average in the Middle East.

From other angles the welfare record is not prepossessing. Infant mortality, estimated at 165 (per 1,000 live births) exceeds even that of Egypt at 118.6. With regard to labor and labor relations, even an approach to the standards prevalent in Western countries remained in abeyance until the beginning of the sixties. In 1936 a basic Labor Code had been enacted with provisions for a 48-hour week, overtime pay, health care, and labor security, but it did not apply to small enterprises, agricultural labor, transport workers, and government employees. Even so, its implementation was postponed by the exigencies of the second world war. The prohibition of strikes and lockouts, however, was enforced until 1963. In general, etatism extended to labor in the sense that anything not expressly permitted was forbidden. Thus it required explicit legislation, such as a Trade Union Act of 1947, to permit the organization of unions in fields not specified in the Labor Code of 1936.

---

[14] Undoubtedly the choice of a western site was influenced also by strategic military considerations.

In 1963 two important pieces of legislation advanced the cause of organized labor: in one act, the confederation of labor unions known as Turk-Is was legally recognized; in another, strikes, in fact recognized as a lawful right by the constitution (article 47), were now permitted by statute, and conditions were laid down for collective agreements. By 1968, of the 14.2 million workers in Turkey, approximately 700,000 (or 5 percent) were members of the existing 1,200 unions. It is interesting to observe that during the history of collective bargaining agreements, involving 9,505 laborers, as many as 3,602 were public employees.

A perennial problem in Turkey, which the first Five Year Development Plan has failed to ameliorate, is unemployment. Its roots rest in surplus labor in agriculture, but its severity in industry is indicated by a current proposal of the industrial unions for shortening the work day to six hours, forcing employers to add another shift in order to maintain the level of production. Unemployment exercises a downward pressure on wages, estimates of the average monthly wage of unskilled urban laborers ranging from TL 300 to TL 550 in 1964, compared to TL 1,000 as a necessary monthly minimum for decent living. Agricultural wages are reported as one-half to one-fourth those of industrial workers, though, of course, allowance must be made for lower costs of living on farms. Thus far no notable progress has been made on the problem of surplus population on the land, estimated by R. D. Robinson at 2 to 2.5 million persons.

Similarly, the acute shortage of urban housing and the huge *gecekondus* (slums or favelas), said to embrace 65 percent of the population of Ankara and 40 percent of Istanbul, have not provoked remedial steps.[15] Summing up, one can say at the minimum that the governments have not, in their eagerness to realize welfare gains, permitted public expenditures for this purpose to outrun the pace of general economic development. The solid gains in national income have gone into the infrastructure, but also—less fortunately—into a doubling of the population over the last three decades. Somewhat belatedly, in 1963, the ban upon the importation and sale of contraceptives was lifted; meanwhile the government has instituted a program for birth control. But, unfortunately, family planning has a relatively low priority in development strategy.

Foreign Trade

Of relative importance, foreign trade normally constitutes not more than 6 or 8 percent of Turkish national income; normally also, the country is self-sufficient in food. Its chief exports are all agricultural, tobacco and cotton vying for first place; its imports are principally machinery, iron, and steel. Both exports and imports go mostly toward the West, especially toward the United States and Germany. But the most critical aspect of the foreign trade is its balance, which was characteristically positive during the twenties and thirties, but which has been strongly negative since 1947. Some illustrative statistics for the recent past follow.

---

[15] *Swiss Review of World Affairs*, March 1969, p. 6.

Turkey: Foreign Trade and Payments

	Unit	1958	1964	1965	1966	1967	1968
Commodity trade	million U.S. $						
Exports f.o.b.	"	247	411	464	490	523	496
Imports c.i.f.	"	−315	−542	−577	−725	−691	−770
Balance	"	−68	−131	−113	−235	−168	−274
Terms of trade	1963 = 100	73	84	74	68	75	78
Export prices		58	92	89	91	98	98
Import prices		80	110	121	133	130	126
Balance of payments	million U.S. $						
Bal. goods and services	"	−86	−89	−20	−95	−74	−212
Private direct investment [a]	"	13	30	29	20	−9	18
Official grants (net)	"	88	16	10	6	6	28
Official loan receipts (net)	"	32	118	136	128	134	150•

[a] Includes other (not direct) private long-term investments on August 20, 1960.

Source: U.S. AID, *Economic Data Book: Near East and South Asia*, Turkey, p. 6, Revision No. 290, November 1969.

Reference to the terms of trade figures reveals that the collapse of Turkish export prices relative to import prices, which in fact goes back to the end of the second world war, is chiefly accountable for the large balance-of-trade deficits. Relative to American types, Turkish tobacco suffered a partial eclipse in popular taste, particularly in Europe; and the postwar decline of the world market dealt a body blow to cotton exports. In the absence of large economic and official aid to Turkey, the balance of payments could only have been brought into equilibrium by a sharp shrinkage of Turkish imports of capital goods and raw materials; economic development would probably have been brought to a halt, unless phenomenal improvements occurred in national productivity.

Turkey was admitted to the Marshall Plan on July 8, 1948, initiating a program of continuous economic and military aid to the present, exceeding by far the help extended to any other Middle East country. Counting in also the two years of postwar relief (1945–48), the total American aid through 1968 (net of repayments and interest) is $5,224.9 million, of which $2,231.3 million has been economic and $2,963.9 million military. The economic portion divides about equally into loans and grants. Turkey has, indeed, received 38.8 percent of American economic and military aid to the Middle East, nearly three times as much as Iran and over six times as much as the third largest recipient, Israel.[16]

American aid funds have gone into farm equipment (chiefly tractors), irrigation, roads and railroads, coal mining (Zonguldak fields), iron, steel and coking facilities

---

[16] Cf. the table on p. 119.

(Karabük), and technical assistance. These investments follow many of the recommendations of the American privately-financed Thornburg Mission of 1949. In the judgment of a study made by the British Royal Institute of International Affairs, they have "played an important role in the post-war advance of Turkey's economy."

In addition to American aid, Turkey has received through 1967 a total of $218 million in assistance from the Communist bloc, $254 million from various international agencies, and—over the years 1960–66—a total of $307 million bilaterally from Germany, the United Kingdom, Italy, and others; these sums amount respectively to 4, 5, and 6 percent, compared with the contribution made by the United States. For purposes of comparison, it may be noted that, during the four years 1964–67, while official loans and grants to Turkey were $554 million, private foreign investment was $94 million, or 17 percent as large.

Had Turkey, for the sake of economic development, too heavily mortgaged the future by contracting foreign debts? It is difficult to answer this question in absolute terms; perhaps the best approach is a comparison of the service of the debt relative to earnings from exports. From the accompanying figures, it will be observed that the

Turkey's Foreign Debt Repayments and Export Earnings

Years	1. Foreign debt service ($ millions)	2. Export earnings ($ millions)	Relative share of 1 in 2 (percent)
1960	92.4	320.7	28.8
1961	132.0	347.1	38.0
1962	145.1	381.2	34.7
1963	145.1	368.1	39.5
1964	141.1	410.8	34.3
1965	172.2	464.0	37.1
1966	146.1	490.0	29.8
1967	132.4	510.0	25.9

Source: Cemal Ziya, "Turkey's Foreign Debts," *Turkish Economic Review*, May–June 1968, pp. 28-35.

absolute amount of the annual debt service expressed in U.S. dollars began to fall in 1964. Partly this resulted from a rise in export earnings, as shown in the preceding table. But in part, it resulted from the fact that, in consequence of the rapid rise of the share of the debt service from 28.8 to 39.5 percent of export earnings from 1960 to 1963, Turkey experienced difficulty in meeting its commitments, leading to the creation of a Consortium by 14 creditor nations, including the United States, in July 1963. The Consortium proceeded to lighten the net annual service charge by, in effect, re-lending a part of it, thus consolidating the debt and lengthening the repayment period.

Undoubtedly it was in large part because of these foreign loans that Turkey could invest $7.2 billion for development during the First Plan period of 1963–67 with an increase of the money supply no greater than 81 percent and a rise of the cost of living (in Istanbul) not exceeding 33 percent for the quinquennium. An optimistic evaluation of the debt operation seems to be warranted by the recent decline in the share of the foreign debt service as a share of export yields. But for this optimism to be continued, the total of foreign debt cannot in the future be expanded unless export earnings rise more than proportionally to it, and unless the present level of external assistance of $125 million annually can be continued for the time being.

Over the period of the First Development Plan, 1963–68, Turkey's exports developed as follows. The poor performance of industry seems to show that internal prices have lost their competitiveness in foreign markets, and this in turn is ascribable in considerable measure to price maintenance for agriculture through deficit financing, to the lag of adjustments of the rate of exchange on the Turkish lira, and to credit and tax policies. An increased share of domestic investment will have to be met by domestic saving, and this involves solving difficult political problems, such as the introduction of effective taxation on agricultural incomes, the continued heavy taxation of business profits, and restraint on the availability of consumers' goods.

Turkey's Exports by Commodity Groups

(in millions of dollars)

Year		Agricultural products	Mining products	Industrial products
1963		284.2	10.6	73.3
1968		399.4	26.0	71.0
	Difference	115.2	15.4	−2.3

Source: Mahmut Seyda, "The Problems of Changing the Structure of Turkey's Exports," *Turkish Economic Review*, May–June 1969, pp. 28–35.

General Appraisal of Turkish Development

Some International Comparisons

One of the most favorable comparisons involves Turkey's average growth rate of GNP in 1966 and 1967 over the preceding year, at 8 percent, with the United Nations table of growth rates in 1960–65 for 58 developing countries. Only seven countries exceeded Turkey's growth, all but one of them in the Middle East.[17] Even if Turkey's growth over the years 1958–68 at 6.4 percent is substituted, only 12 countries in the world registered greater rates over the 1965 period—about one-fifth of the list.

Limiting the comparisons to the Asiatic Middle East plus the United Arab Republic, one finds Turkey's per capita GNP at $296 in 1966 to be less than one-tenth of Kuwait's or one-fifth of Israel's slightly over Iran and Iraq at $252 and $268 respectively, and substantially ahead of Egypt at $168. With respect to population growth, Turkey and Egypt paired off at 2.4 and 2.5 percent increase per annum, between such extremes as Iran at 3.3 and Israel at 2.0. Literacy stood at 47 percent in Turkey, Kuwait at the same level, with Yemen at 10 percent and Israel at 90 percent in 1966.[18]

---

[17] U.S. AID, *Economic Data Book: Near East and South Asia*, NESA, Revision No. 274, October 1968; United Nations, *World Economic Survey* 1967, Part I, Table 4.
[18] U.S. AID, *op. cit.*, Revision No. 277, December 1968.

The annual growth rate achieved in agriculture by Turkey was 3 percent (1963–67), which was approximately the mode among 58 developing countries. For industry, the same comparison is 9.1 percent for Turkey, and a mode for other developing countries of about 7 percent.[19]

Finally, life expectancy at birth, given at five-year intervals beginning in 1945 and extending through 1965 rose as follows: 46.3, 52.7, 55.7, and 57.6, a creditable improvement in a score of years.[20]

What the Republic Symbolizes

From statistical comparisons such as these, there emerges an economic record for Turkey which is very good in certain ways, average in some, but poor only exceptionally. The mere assembling of "cold figures" is, however, apt to miss the spiritual side which supplies the driving force of development. Thinking primarily of the first two decades of the history of the Republic, Herschlag writes: "From the historical point of view, the republican-étatist regime accomplished a first-rate task. It consolidated the young state, disposed quite rapidly of many of the social and religious traditions of the Ottoman Empire, gradually cancelled out the negative aspects of the Lausanne Treaty, and laid the foundations for progress in the social and economic spheres."[21]

There has, furthermore, been a certain improvement in the economic level of the peasants through rural credit, land distribution, and price supports; road-building and other communication media have improved village life; education has raised the tone of local entrepreneurship.

A recent retrospect leads Richard D. Robinson to conclude: "First, the Turks have been trying—with a startling measure of success—to make the transition from authoritarianism to liberalism with a minimum of political violence. Second, Turkey is deeply involved in explosive economic development. Third, Turkey has emerged as a modern military power."[22]

Looking forward after nearly 50 years of history, what are the chief assets and liabilities of this nation from the viewpoint of its further economic evolution?

Weakness and Strength for Development

Most of Turkey's economic handicaps are typical of underdeveloped countries. Amongst them, first mention should go to the demographic problem, which diluted the excellent 6.4 percent annual increase of GNP during the decade 1958–68 to a per capita value of 2.3 percent. Turkey's 2.4 percent annual rate of population increase is exceeded by many underdeveloped countries, but this country's modern orientation should be reflected in a lower birthrate. Its record of infant mortality at 165 per thousand reveals a sad wastage of human and economic values.

[19] U.S. AID, *op. cit.*, Turkey, Revision No. 266, June 1968; United Nations, *op. cit.*, Table 6.

[20] Republic of Turkey, State Planning Organization, *Second Five Year Development Plan, 1968–1972* (Ankara: Central Bank of the Republic of Turkey, 1969).

[21] Herschlag, *Turkey, An Economy in Transition* (The Hague: van Keulen, n.d.), p. 172.

[22] Robinson, *The First Turkish Republic, op. cit.*, Preface, p. vii.

Something similar is to be said of inflation, where—as we have seen—the cost of living rose by 33 percent over five years through 1967, an amount which seems less shocking in comparison with Latin America and many other countries. However, the government's problems of rational price fixing, its difficulty in curbing the demand for consumer goods, as well as the general problem of encouraging domestic saving and investment—all these are complicated by inflation. Indeed, the availability of consumer goods has been characterized as the one most important political issue.

Very serious also are the numerous problems which beset the State Economic Enterprises, now controlling the big industrial and mining units, the railroads and other shipping facilities, and the major financial organizations. They entail a heavy drain on the budget and are a major inflationary factor. "Their problems, ranging from overemployment to poor management, to uneconomic activities and uneconomic locations have meant a very low return per unit of capital in industry, major distortions of the price structure, and much protection for inefficiencies in the private sector." [23]

Finally, to single out only conspicuous channels of possible improvement, are the shortcomings of the educational system, despite successes in raising the level of literacy. Primary and secondary school curricula are antiquated and the universities are too little oriented toward turning out technically trained scientists and managers for a developing economy. [24]

On the side of strength, Turkey has been vouchsafed a stability in its government which is rare in the annals of young developing countries. Only twice, in 1950 and 1964, since the founding of the Republic in 1923, has the party in power been displaced; and only once, in 1960, did civilian give place to military authority. Subsequently, however, the military attenuated its role to a sort of watchdog, while civilians functioned at all levels of government. Complaints are sometimes heard that the government, while professing its interest in a thriving private enterprise sector, has done nothing to forward it. It is indeed true that the Democrat party, in power since 1950 (with a four-year interruption, 1960–64) generally has continued the policies of the Republican party. But the very stability of the etatist regime has favored the development of private enterprise, and many of the ablest private industrial engineers and economists have come up in state industries. The compatibility of Turkish etatism and private undertakings is perhaps indicated by the fact that the period of most rapid industrial growth, 1960–63, saw an increase in private employment from 72,000 to 102,000. while government employment gained only from 75,000 to 82,000.

The second major strength of the Turkish economy lies in its natural resource base: agricultural land of a quality and quantity to assure food self-sufficiency at the least, and an ample endowment of coal and iron reserves for the further development of heavy industry, unique in the Middle East. Furthermore, the richness of agricultural and industrial raw materials is complemented by a large population. Only three countries of the Middle East had a population in the 1960s in excess of 20 million—Turkey with 34 million, the United Arab Republic with 31 million, Iran with 26 million—while all others (Afghanistan with 14 million excepted), had populations of 10 million or less. One may perhaps question whether a certain minimum population

---

[23] Commission on International Development, *op. cit.*, p. 320.
[24] Richard D. Robinson, *High-Level Manpower in Economic Development: The Turkish Case* (Cambridge: Harvard University Press, 1967)

can be laid down as the *sine qua non* of self-sustaining economic growth. But there can be little question that a strong domestic market offers advantages. With only 6–7 percent of its GNP in foreign trade, Turkey is already launched on the more stable course of production for the home market. To realize its full potential implies that, along with industrialization, agricultural productivity, and farm incomes must increase also.

IV. LEBANON: PRIVATE ENTERPRISE

Distinctive Character

Lebanon is the smallest of the Arab countries in the Middle East, with an area about equal to the Yellowstone National Park of the United States; it is also the most densely populated, with an estimated 2,810,000 inhabitants in 1969. But there are other, more noteworthy, attributes of this small nation: the highest standard of living in the Arab world, the lowest rate of illiteracy, the largest proportion of educated women, the lowest percentage of persons in agriculture, and the highest per capita national income in the Middle East ($633 in 1967), aside from Israel and Kuwait.[1]

These distinctions have been achieved without domestic sources of oil, without great and fertile river valleys, and—despite the extreme dependence of the country on foreign trade—without even a good port. "It is generally agreed," writes Professor Issawi of Columbia University, "that this remarkable development has been achieved by the enterprise of private Lebanese citizens, and has owed little to the help of either nature, or foreigners, or the government."[2] Something in the neighborhood of 80 percent of investment over several decades down to the mid-1950s was private in origin.[3]

One could point to further characteristics of the Lebanese economy and society which are unique: the prevalence of free trade and the absence of exchange control, the maintenance of price level stability (after an inflationary episode during the second world war), the large emigration of traders to America—chiefly to the United States and Brazil—the quantitative importance of emigrants' remittances to the homeland, and finally the existence of a substantial middle class. But the most important economic feature has been the private enterprise economy, which underlies many, if not most, of the attributes. What accounts for the vigor and persistence of private investment and entrepreneurship?

---

[1] Peretz, *op. cit.*, p. 317; and U.S. AID, *Economic Data Book, Near East and South Asia*, NESA Regional, pp. 6, 7. Revision No. 277, December 1968.

[2] Charles Issawi, "Economic Development and Liberalism in Lebanon," *The Middle East Journal*, Summer 1964, p. 280.

[3] A. J. Meyer, *Middle Eastern Capitalism* (Cambridge: Harvard University Press, 1959), pp. 22, 46.

Probably their most remote origins historically lie in the facts that the ancient Phoenicians, living on a crossroads of the world, became the greatest traders of their age, and that trade has always been a private enterprise field *par excellence*. Another undoubtedly very basic factor has been the nature of the agriculture. Professor Issawi points out that, in contrast with Egypt and Mesopotamia where vast systems of irrigation required centralized planning and control, in Lebanon the agriculture is rain-fed, a condition conducive to farming by independent individuals.[4] Another factor has been the influence of the Christian missionary schools which, at an early juncture in modern history, instilled Western ideas of democracy and free enterprise. Ideas and ideals of this sort have also been supplied by Lebanese entrepreneurs who have emigrated to the New World and who have returned to their native heath imbued with Western attitudes. Finally, a not inconsiderable factor has been the relative paucity of foreigners in control of domestic finance, trade, and production in Lebanon, which has developed its own business class.

Historical Notes

Herodotus, the venerable "father of history," wrote that he would devote as much attention to small countries as to great, and the economic peculiarities of Lebanon just described would be ample warrant for giving heed to its history. But here practically nothing can be said of that fascinating history which extends through Babylonian, Persian, Greek, Roman, Crusading, and Ottoman times.[5] Through most of its history, Lebanon has been an independent or semi-independent merchant republic; and much of its history is linked with that of the Maronite Christian sect, founded by the monk John Maron in the eighth century. The sect came into special favor with the Roman popes and in 1250 was accorded French protection by Louis IX. Thus began an association which accounts for the prevalence of the French language and culture in Lebanon, the French mandate from 1919 to the end of the second world war and even the first systematic economic study of the country, *Le Liban Face à Son Développement*, made in 1960–61 by the Institut de Récherches et de Formation en vue du Développement, of Paris.

It was in 1860, after a clash between the Maronites and the Druses, that the Ottoman sultan established Lebanon as an independent province governed by a council with a membership divided out among the six principal religious sects. Government based upon representation by religion, adopted in 1861, has continued to the present day, supplemented by an unwritten National Pact in 1943 in which it was assumed that the Christians had a majority. Even after the revolution of 1958, seats in the parliament have always been based on a ratio of six Christians to five Muslims. By custom, the president is a Maronite Christian, the premier a Sunni Muslim, and the president of the Chamber a Shiah Muslim.[6]

During the long and peaceful period of autonomy from 1864 to 1914, the government pursued a policy of noninterference in economic matters, though it constructed

---

[4] Charles Issawi, "Social Structure and Ideology in Iraq, Lebanon, and the UAR," in Thompson and Reischauer, *op. cit.*, p. 145.

[5] The great work on the subject is Philip K. Hitti, *Lebanon in History* (London: Macmillan, 3d ed., 1967).

[6] Much of the historical account is based upon Hitti, *ibid.*, Peretz, *op. cit.*, and Issawi, *op. cit.*

a highway network unmatched in the region. Business interests enjoyed a low level of taxation unequaled in neighboring countries. The first world war, however, brought disaster to Lebanon through the tie of its currency with the French franc and through the collapse of its silk industry.[7] But Lebanese enterprise soon found an escape through the replacing of mulberries by fruit trees; and during the thirties, the tourist trade began to flourish. Early in the first world war, the French established a *de facto* sovereignty for themselves which was converted into an official mandate by the League of Nations in 1922. The interwar period was generally an unhappy one for the Lebanese. "Mandatory officials were often corrupt, avaricious and arbitrary . . . public services lagged behind those in the British Palestine mandate."[8] But the French maintained law and order, built roads and schools, improved standards of public health, and Beirut came to be a leading Mediterranean port.

In contrast with the first, the second world war brought certain gains to Lebanon. Allied expenditure from 1939 through 1944 in Syria and Lebanon produced a balance-of-payments surplus of Syrian £607 million, attended, however, by a terrific inflation; in Beirut wholesale prices rose from 100 in June 1939, to 1,203 in January 1945. But the money reserves of financiers, merchants, and industrialists rose by $100 million. Beirut became the financial center of the Middle East and one of the leading trade centers of the world. "Fabulous, yet perfectly authentic, stories are told of the transfer of gold from Mexico to India and China, of the shipment of copper from Franco's Spain to Stalin's Russia, and of the sale of a huge consignment of toothbrushes from an Italian firm to a neighboring one—and all directed from some mangy-looking business house in Beirut."[9]

We have mentioned the abandoning of silk production from mulberry trees and the switch to fruit orchards, in and following the first world war. The long-run gains of this change are shown in the following figures:

Fruit Production and Agricultural Income in Lebanon

	1948–52	1958–60
Apples in tons	14,000	54,000
Citrus in tons	75,000	146,000
Bananas in tons	16,000	3,000
Agricultural income in millions of Lebanese £	206 (1950)	380 (1960)

Source: Issawi, p. 286.

This near doubling of agricultural income in a decade was approximated in other fields during somewhat shorter or longer periods. All of this added up to a rise in national income from L£ 1,042 million in 1950 to L£ 1,503 million in 1957 (the year

[7] Recently, however, steps have been taken to rehabilitate mulberry farming and the silk industry. *Los Angeles Times*, January 1, 1970.
[8] Peretz, *op. cit.*, p. 323.
[9] Issawi, "Economic Development . . . ," *op. cit.*, p. 284.

before the revolution), a 50 percent rise in seven years or an average of about 7 percent annually in uncorrected monetary terms, during which period the wholesale price index in Beirut *declined* by nearly one-fifth![10]

Activity in Other Fields in the Fifties in Lebanon

Number of industrial enterprises	2,604 (1956)	3,302 (1960)
Industrial capital, millions of L£	213 "	436 "
Industrial labor force	22,000 "	39,000 "
Output of electricity, millions of kwh	164 (1953)	350 "
Output of cement, in tons	314,000 "	854,000 "
Number of tourists	89,000 (1951)	233,000 "

Source: Issawi, *op. cit.*, p. 286.

While this rapid rate of economic development was being achieved, political developments were less fortunate, though by no means as troubled as they came to be after 1958. By an agreement of the U.S., USSR, Great Britain, and France in 1946, the troops of the latter two nations were withdrawn from Lebanon and Syria, which thereby became free and independent. In Lebanon, President Bishara al Khuri was displaced in the so-called "Rose Water Revolution" of September 1952. Camille Chamoun was elected president. The Communist party was made illegal for all of this decade and, under various fronts, was generally defeated in parliamentary elections. But the really burning issues were the pro- and anti-Nasser question and the closely-related problem of Lebanon vis-à-vis Israel and the Western powers. In July 1958, when the Hashemite regime in Iraq was overthrown, rioting broke out in Beirut, and President Chamoun requested and obtained the intervention of American troops under the "Eisenhower Doctrine"; they restored order without untoward incident and withdrew by the end of the year. After this abortive "revolution," the Lebanon government continued, under the religious-political compromise, to enforce more or less the status quo.

During the sixties, part of the political trouble in Lebanon can be ascribed to Arab impatience with the continuance of the 6:5 Christian-Arab ratio in the parliament and official positions. The Christians feared that Nasser or the Baath socialist revolutionaries in Syria would engineer an Arab scheme for unity which would reduce them to an impotent minority. With the issue of the Palestinian commandos' use of Lebanon as a base of operations against Israel as a pretext, Syria shut off the oil flow to Tripoli in December 1966, for a period of several months, reducing Lebanese petroleum production by half.

In October 1969, much greater damage was done to the economy of Lebanon by the closing of the Syrian border, which halted that country's transit trade to the East, with Syria, Iraq, Kuwait, Jordan, and Saudi Arabia. This involved the larger part of

---

[10] United Nations, *Statistical Yearbooks*.

the $300 million annual transit trade of Lebanon with the Arab world. At the same time, tourist traffic declined by 40 percent. There can be little doubt that the political issues of Arab countries with Lebanon are being made the occasion for measures to destroy the bourgeois government of the country. During the sixties, the United States sharply curtailed aid to Lebanon, which may be led to turn instead to the USSR.

Foreign Trade and Finance

Lebanon is a commercial nation twice compounded. In the first place, commerce accounted in 1966 for as much as 31 percent of the GNP. In the second place, imports substantially exceed exports, the deficit being covered by transit dues, services to foreigners, emigrant remittances, and the tourist trade. While the trade deficit has been decried as a "growing imbalance,"[11] the more sophisticated view holds the deficit to be a necessity—indeed, a symptom of prosperity and a factor favorable to development.[12] It is estimated that productivity per unit of labor in Lebanon is one-third the national average in agriculture and construction, about equal to the average in industry, but 2.8 times the average in commerce and 15 times in finance.[13] But it has to be conceded that the economic gains of foreign trade are purchased with a growing economic and political vulnerability, symbolized by the constant increase of the trade deficit since 1953.

Imports, which have increased by 10 percent per annum since 1960, are generally free of duty except for revenue purposes, and import licensing is limited to a few items, such as wheat, olive oil, leather bags, which could compete with local products. Imports are concentrated on foodstuffs, construction materials, textiles, and equipment. Exports from Lebanon have grown by threefold since 1960 but suffice to pay for only one-fifth of the value of imports. Industrial exports, though increasing, are still relatively small; agricultural exports are chiefly citrus fruits, apples, bananas, vegetables, and, lately, poultry, which has developed into a $30 million business annually.[14]

Chief among the invisible exports, which combine to pay for Lebanon's import balance, is the transit trade, amounting to $300 million per annum. While part of this large total arises from a diversion of trade which used to travel through the Suez Canal before its closure, Lebanon possesses skilled labor and good storage facilities for the entrepôt trade, a more permanent advantage. However, three-fourths of the transit trade is involved in the movement of petroleum in the Tapline and IPC pipelines to Sidon and Tripoli, which are subject to the political vicissitudes of Syria, Lebanon's neighbor to the east. In addition to the transit trade, reexports earn $35 million for the country, among which are refined petroleum and the substantial trade in gold.

Second among invisible exports comes tourism, providing $80 million or 18 percent of Lebanon's total foreign earnings in 1966 (7–8 percent of GNP), resulting from an increase in the number of foreign visitors by 20 percent annually since 1960. While the

---

[11] Issawi, "Economic Development . . . ," op. cit., p. 289.

[12] Institut de Formation en vue du Développement, Le Liban Face à son Développement (Beirut, 1963), p. 249; hereafter referred to as Institut.

[13] Institut, p. 215.

[14] This and other trade information is given in the excellent special country report on Lebanon in The Chase Manhattan Bank, N.A., World Business, No. 12, July 1968, pp. 17–23.

attractions of the country's beaches, ski resorts, and archaeological sites are more or less permanent, the tourist trade is subject to episodic disturbance, as, for example, in 1967 in consequence of the Arab-Israeli war.

Among the remaining items in the invisible export category are income from Lebanese foreign investments at $25 million a year, remittances from overseas Lebanese at $35 million, and payment of a lesser but important total for the services of Lebanese bankers, stock brokers, exchange dealers, and insurance companies, which have earned for the country the reputation of the "Switzerland of the Arab world." [15] The foreign investments and the emigrants' remittances arise from generations of Lebanese now numbering a million, who have become entrepreneurs and capitalists in foreign countries, principally in Brazil and the United States. According to semiofficial estimates, this emigration amounted to 3,000 annually from 1860 to 1900; 15,000 per year from 1900 to 1914; 4,400 from 1921 to 1939; and 3,000 from 1945 to the present.

In concluding on Lebanon's trade and finance, it may be pointed out that, while these items involved about a third of the country's GNP, the amount of employment they provide does not exceed 10 percent of the total, according to United Nations figures. Finally, it is estimated that about 50 percent of Lebanon's exports currently go to neighboring Arab countries, while the United States, France, West Germany, and Syria are the principal suppliers of its imports.

Agriculture

About two-thirds of the population is involved with agriculture, but perhaps not more than one-tenth of the national income emanates from this source.[16] From these facts alone, it is obvious that the rural people do not share much in the prosperity of the commercial and financial sectors. As remarked earlier, labor productivity in agriculture is estimated at one-third the national average; farming methods are primitive. Nevertheless, authorities agree that the standard of living on the land is superior to that of Greece and southern Italy. Similarly, while the distribution of land ownership is extremely unequal, the agricultural population has a much higher proportion of free-holding cultivators than neighboring countries.[17] In absolute terms, the total production of Lebanese farming has risen over the years 1958–67 from an index of 96 (1957–59 = 100) to 204, though it experienced a setback in 1968 to 175 because of the Arab-Israeli war.[18] This doubling of output is attributable to the spread of mechanized farming, the increase of cash crops, and improvement of marketing facilities.[19] Land reform is regarded as an essential to further progress, through improving the motivation and the amenities of rural life, as well as allowing more saving by the cultivators and investment in farm apparatus.

---

[15] In 1966 the country was shaken by the failure of its largest commercial bank, the Intra Bank. Banking reform measures adopted subsequently have nearly restored the pre-Intra level of confidence.

[16] Don Peretz, "River Schemes and the Effect on Economic Development in Jordan, Syria, and Lebanon," *The Middle East Journal*, Summer 1964, p. 301.

[17] In 1948, holdings of 13 acres or less constituted 98.6 percent of all land ownership, while 1 percent of the holdings embraced half of the total agricultural land. Berger, *op. cit.*, p. 197; Hitti, *op. cit.*, p. 503.

[18] U.S. AID, *Economic Data Book, Near East and South Asia*, Lebanon, p. 5. Revision No. 290, November 1969.

[19] Fuad I. Khuri, "The Changing Class Structure in Lebanon," *The Middle East Journal*, Winter 1969, p. 36.

Of great importance for the future also is the Litani River project, which is expected to add 30 percent to the irrigated acreage upon its completion in 1975 and to add to the electric generating capacity of the country, presently dependent in part upon imported oil. Part of the cost of this project is defrayed from a $27 million loan made in August 1955, by the International Bank. Complementing the Litani scheme, the Lebanese government has launched a five-year program of rural development in roads, drinking water, irrigation, and electricity costing L£ 450 million. All of this promises to strengthen a relatively neglected sector of the economy; but a limit to agricultural expansion is set by the fact that 70 percent of the country's area is mountainous.

Industry

While Lebanese agriculture absorbs about two-thirds of the labor force and turns out only 10 percent of the national income, industry—claiming only 10 percent of the labor force (or 65,000 employees)—accounts for an estimated 15 percent of national income. In fact, no general measure of industrial output exists, but the estimate seems plausible. Furthermore, industry in Lebanon, until recently at least, has shown a very lively rate of increase, estimated at 9.5 percent per annum from 1961 to 1966.[20] Again, the estimate does not seem exaggerated when compared with general industrial indicators, such as cement production, increasing by 8 percent annually 1958–68, and new construction, increasing by 25.6 percent annually 1961–66. However, both of these series and the GNP registered reversals in 1967 and 1968, the latest available statistics. But in exports, even these years were good years for industry: having doubled from $15 to $30 million 1964–67, they continued this pace in the first quarter of 1968.

The rise of industry in Lebanon begins to make good for its retardation under the French mandate, which did everything to discourage native competition with industrial imports from France.[21] For many years industry suffered from the restricted domestic market and high rates of interest. But in July 1954, the government of the republic exempted new industrial establishments, under certain conditions, from the income tax and from customs duties on machinery and raw materials; and a newly founded Agriculture and Real Estate Bank was also authorized to grant limited credits to industry.

Food processing, textiles, and other consumer goods dominate Lebanon's industries, but there are two steel rolling mills. At Sidon and at Tripoli two refineries, belonging respectively to the Mediterranean Refining Company and the Iraq Petroleum Company, have input capacities of 800,000 and 1,200,000 tons of petroleum. Both are wholly dependent upon the flow of oil through pipelines traversing Syria from the Kirkuk fields in northern Iraq. Usually excluded from statistical statements of "industry" is the production of electrical energy. From 1958 to 1968 output in this sector rose from 290 million kwh to 1,035 million, a 25.7 percent increase annually. In 1958 the ratio of thermal to hydroelectric generation was slightly more than 1:1, thus Lebanon is pretty much at the mercy of oil from the East unless it substantially increases its hydroelectric generation or derives oil from other sources, a politically hazardous alternative.

---

[20] Chase National Bank, *op. cit.*, p. 21.
[21] *Institut*, pp. 239–40.

Evaluation and Conclusions

One unfortunate consequence of Lebanon's rapid economic development is said to be a marked increase in inequality. Possibly, as Professor Issawi suggests, this is "a natural concomitant of economic development carried out in a liberal framework . . . perhaps the main driving force behind the opposition to economic liberalism." [22] Professor Simon Kuznets has argued that this situation characterized the economic history of the United Kingdom from 1780 to 1850, of the United States and Germany from 1840 to 1890, and of Israel since 1948. Be that as it may, some 18 percent of the population of Lebanon receive incomes above the mean, while for such developed countries as Denmark, the United States, and Italy the figure runs from 25 to 40 percent, indicating a wider sharing of easy circumstances. [23]

In this context, however, it would be wise to observe that the less-developed countries *in general* reveal a greater inequality of wealth and income than the developed countries, and that Lebanon's 18 percent who are above average income far exceed those of, say, Colombia with only 8 percent. Secondly, the measurement of inequality by a sophisticated device such as the Lorenz curve is usually impossible in less developed countries because of the lack of data, and one is thrown back on the general observation of reputable authorities such as Professor Issawi or the *Institut*, which are, however, not infallible. Finally, inequality might increase while general economic welfare for everyone increases, and that would appear to be very probable for Lebanon. This does not, of course, apologize for a lack of equalitarian measures, if such be the case. It is notable in this respect that Sheik Najib Alamuddin, manager of the largest private business in the Middle East, Middle East Airlines, acknowledged the problem and strongly advised that in order for Lebanon to continue developing, private enterprise there should recognize the need for a more equitable distribution of wealth. [24]

Another complaint by a foreign observer has been the rapidity of population increase in Lebanon. At an annual rate of 2.4 percent, the increase is moderate compared to 3.0 in Jordan, 3.3 in Iran, and 3.5 in Kuwait, but about the same as in Turkey or Egypt. For all of these—and many more—countries, it would not be unreasonable to apply the presently popular ideal of "zero population increase" in order not to see the economic development being achieved dissipated by the head count. With Lebanon's narrow resource base, the rule would be especially desirable for the country's well-being.

On other welfare matters, Lebanon's record is better or outstanding. Most notable, perhaps, is labor legislation, which includes an eight-hour day in industry, maternity and sick leave, prohibition of child labor, and requirements for safety in factories. But not much has been done in the general field of social security. Public health conditions are good, the mortality rate of 5.4 per cent (1953) being one of the lowest in the Middle East, and the infant mortality rate (early sixties) being the lowest, Israel excepted in both cases. The numbers of inhabitants per hospital bed and per physician follow the same pattern.

[22] Issawi, "Economic Development . . . ," *op. cit.*, p. 287.

[23] *Institut*, p. 215.

[24] Sheik Najib Alamuddin, "The Role of Private Enterprise in the Economic Development of the Middle East." Address before the 20th anniversary conference of the Middle East Institute, Washington, 1966.

In the field of education, Lebanon has the lowest illiteracy rate and the highest proportion of educated women in the Arab world, as previously pointed out. Practically all children of primary school age actually attend, compared to about 50 percent for the region as a whole. Beirut prides itself on three institutions of higher learning: the University of Lebanon with 2,600 students (1960), St. Joseph's College with 1,900, and the American University, which draws nearly 4,000 students from all countries of the Middle East.

Finally, for human welfare, scarcely the least important matters are two which are sometimes overlooked. First, is the virtual absence of inflation; the wholesale price index rose over the decade 1958–68 by 10 percent, i.e., one percent per annum, a record scarcely to be equaled anywhere. Or, perhaps more accurately and more dramatically, unequaled when combined with a second welfare phenomenon, a virtual absence of unemployment.[25]

The rate of increase of gross national product, estimated at 4.4 percent per annum in the fifties and 4 percent in the sixties, falls short by 1 to 2 percent of the other countries of the present study. It stands somewhat in a middle position between the rapidly advancing countries of the Middle East, the more slowly progressing nations of Latin America, and the still more sedate pace of the "already developed" nations of the industrial world. With its high per capita income of $633, the highest in the Middle East at the latest accounting, aside from Israel and Kuwait, Lebanon in fact stands between the categories of underdeveloped and developed, and its increase of national income accords with this fact.

Whether the accomplishments of this small country can be attributed to its general free enterprise character or not is, of course, subject to debate. Noting that public investment formed 15 percent of the total in 1952–54 and 30 percent in 1959, one writer remarked, "Lebanon has thus come a long way from its traditional *laissez-faire* policy"; but it is the same observer who declares that the country's remarkable record has been achieved by the enterprise of its private citizens.[26] Beyond any doubt has been the prevalence of free trade and the general absence of exchange controls, as well as the posture of noninterference in business and commercial affairs. Thus far also no question has been raised as to whether parliamentary government survives without police-state support.

An American business journal sets forth what it considers to be those aspects of Lebanon's economic success which are relevant to other less-developed nations: investment in human resources to upgrade living standards; fair and equal treatment of foreign investors; liberal policies and free markets for local enterprise; stable prices and stable currencies.[27] But there is also general agreement that Lebanon's mercantile and financial services by which it earns its essential imports, the markets for its rather special agricultural products, its entrepôt trade, even the inflow of petroleum for its refineries and electric power—all these are very vulnerable to political or economic interference from abroad. Its economy was constructed for a peaceful world and it can live only in that setting.

---

[25] U.S. AID, *Economic Data Book, Near East and South Asia*, Lebanon, p. 4. Revision No. 288, September 1969.

[26] Issawi, "Economic Development . . .," *op. cit.*, pp. 280, 290.

[27] Chase Manhattan Bank, *op. cit.*, p. 23.

V. IRAN: PRIVATE ENTERPRISE
ASSISTED BY THE STATE

Beginning about 1954 Iran has been caught up in an industrial revolution and a general economic upsurge of unprecedented proportions. Even during the several years when the oil industry was recovering from the crisis produced by nationalization in 1951, the economy began to move ahead. Among the main industrial and mining products, for example, cement production rose from 131 to 700 thousand tons from 1955 to 1959, sugar from 75 to 110, chromite from 10 to 46; and cotton textiles from 34 to 160 thousand meters.[1] This was, however, only a prelude to the rapid and sustained economic development which has followed. In the decade 1958–68, gross national product (deflated to 1967 prices) increased steadily by an average of 9 percent yearly, while per capita real income—despite the 3.2 per thousand annual increase of population—rose on the average by 4.2 percent![2]

The character of the economic system under which this phenomenal advance has taken place is well indicated in the following words of Professor Charles Issawi: "While government was thus laying the infrastructure, private enterprise was building the structure."[3] Beside the generally smooth functioning of government departments, the vision of the Shah and several of his ministers contributed to this process, as did also the rich endowment of the country in petroleum resources, the help of foreign governments, including the United States and later Russia, and the cooperation of the oil companies. A brief historical retrospect will reveal, however, that the successes of the past decade have come only after many troubled years for the country.

Historical Note

The land of the Medes and Persians reached its greatest eminence in the sixth century B.C. Achaemenian Empire, which was overthrown by Alexander the Great in 334–330 B.C. Thereafter, Persia was subjected to succeeding invasions by Arabs,

---

[1] George B. Baldwin, *Planning and Development in Iran* (Baltimore: The Johns Hopkins Press, 1967), p. 10.
[2] U.S. AID, *Economic Data Book, Near East and South Asia*, Iran, p. 2, Revision No. 280, March 1969.
[3] Charles Issawi, "Iran's Economic Upsurge," *The Middle East Journal*, Autumn 1967, p. 449.

Turks, and Mongols. During the Middle Ages, it is said, Persia existed not as a country but only as a geographical expression. In the nineteenth century, the history of the country was written largely in terms of the rivalry of the Great Powers, chiefly Britain and Russia.[4] The first world war made Persia a battleground for Turkish, Russian, and British forces. Russia maintained pressure on the country in the postwar period, withdrawing only in 1921 after winning a concession of the Caspian fisheries.

After the second world war, the USSR signed a tripartite alliance with Iran and Britain in 1942, and undertook "to respect the territorial integrity, sovereignty, and political independence of Iran," but then proceeded to interfere with Persian officials, police, and troops.[5] In the postwar scene, the Communist Tudeh party combined with the radical left wing to support USSR machinations and demands for oil concessions. Taking advantage of indecision on the part of the western powers, Iranian Communists of a rich agricultural border province, supported by the Red army, proclaimed an "Autonomous Republic of Azerbaijan" in December 1945. Not until the premier of Iran had cleared his cabinet of Communist members could he send troops into Azerbaijan, whereupon the secessionist regime collapsed.[6]

The foundations of modern Iran were laid by the redoubtable Reza Shah, a trooper and later officer of the Iranian Cossack Division, who brought about a coup d'état in 1921, and who quickly became commander-in-chief and subsequently minister of war. Reza Shah put down rebellions in the provinces, defeated Communist elements and was crowned king in 1926. He introduced the French judicial system, decreed universal compulsory primary education, abolished the Muslim veil for women, introduced public health measures, and founded the University of Teheran. In general, economic matters were left to private initiative, though a foreign trade monopoly was created as a measure of defense against the USSR. While Reza Shah was responsible for setting up a number of factories, most of them did not prove to be viable in the long run. Far and away his most significant economic contribution was the construction, between 1927 and 1939, of the Trans-Iranian Railroad, financed by taxes on tea and sugar. Also the mission of an American, Dr. Arthur Millspaugh, from 1922 to 1927, brought order into the country's domestic finances. Finally in 1941, as a consequence of British and Soviet invasions, Reza Shah abdicated, a monumental but controversial figure.

Acceding to the throne, the youthful Mohammed Reza Pahlavi entered a scene marked by war and postwar disruptions, political assassinations, and the rebellions of the Kurds. In 1947, President Truman pledged military assistance to Greece and Turkey and, some months later, an American military mission went to Iran and grants of $26 million were extended for military equipment. The engineering firm of Morrison Knudsen, of Boise, Idaho, conducted an economic survey in 1947 which became the basis of Iran's first Seven Year Development Plan, 1948–55. A visit of the Shah to the United States in 1949 failed to produce aid on a scale which he and many of his countrymen had anticipated. This reversal, coupled with anti-foreign activities of the Fayaden Islam, resulted in a nationalization of the oil industry in 1951 and the rule

---

[4] Donald N. Wilber, *Iran, Past and Present* (Princeton, N.J.: Princeton University Press, 5th ed., 1963), Chapter II.
[5] Royal Institute of International Affairs, *op. cit.*, pp. 378–79.
[6] George Lenczowski, *The Middle East in World Affairs* (Ithaca, N.Y.: Cornell University Press, 3d ed., 1962), pp. 194–97.

of the violent patriot Mossadegh for two periods as prime minister before his downfall in August 1953. With the termination of the oil stoppage in 1954, Iran turned a corner; but recovery from the "political trauma" produced by Mossadegh and from the setback of the oil industry required several years.

By the time of the coronation of the Shah in 1967, the country had surmounted the last of a series of shocks it had suffered from the first world war on. As Professor Issawi points out, the Shah contributed significantly to the reestablishment of popular confidence by his leadership in land reform, his interest in economic and social development, and—not least—his skillful handling of relations with the Soviet Union, which opened up new markets and unlocked a huge source of capital.[7]

Despite constitutional limits to the Shah's powers, he controls the army, selects half the members of the Senate, may introduce and veto legislation, and in emergency may suspend individual rights and freedoms. Thus it is apparent that the character of the Shah is a critical matter. Fortunately for the nation, the present monarch's qualities are a major factor in its political stability and economic progress over the past 15 years. Indeed, his "White Revolution," inaugurated in 1963 and adopted by a popular referendum, has produced greater practical results than economic planning, to which we turn next. In a mixture of economic, political, and welfare measures, the sixfold White Revolution offers a powerful program to reduce inequality, better the material and nonmaterial lot of the common man, and build morale.

The economic ingredients of the Six Point Reform Program are three: land reform and the nationalization of the forests, which have practically abolished the landlord class; popular sharing of ownership in the state industries; and profit sharing in industry generally. On the political side, all citizens including women are guaranteed a share in the sovereignty of government by the new election laws and the Equity Courts offer to all citizens the protection of legal "due process." Finally the organization of the Literacy Corps and Health Corps contributes essential elements to human welfare. The economic side of these notable reforms will be observed in subsequent parts on the major sectors of the Iranian economy.

The Economic Plans

If economic planning has been overshadowed by the Shah's White Revolution, this is not for want of able economic and other experts, both native and foreign, nor for lack of financial resources except for the period of the oil crisis. As early as 1922, as already noted, an expert from the United States was entrusted with surveying the economic scene and recommending measures. Planning has undergone a gradual crescendo down to the present plan. Even before the first plan, revenues of the Anglo-Iranian Oil Company helped to support public projects, and oil royalties have contributed huge sums thereafter.

First Seven Year Plan, 1948–55

Based upon the Morrison Knudsen report of 1947, this plan contemplated a total expenditure of 26.3 billion rials or $650 million, to be largely financed by oil revenues from the AIOC. Planned and actual expenditures were as follows. As a result of the

---

[7] Issawi, "Iran's Economic Upsurge," *op. cit.*, p. 448.

Planned and Actual Expenditures of the First Plan

| | Planned | | Actual |
	in percent	in billion rials	in billion rials
Agriculture and irrigation	27.8	7.3	5.7
Transport and communications	29.3	7.7	3.5
Industries and mines	20.1	5.3	4.1
Social services	22.8	6.0	0.8
Total	100.0	26.3	14.1

Source: *Quarterly Economic Review, Iran, Annual Supplement 1969* (London: The Economist Intelligence Unit Ltd.), p. 4.

1951–55 oil crisis only 54 percent of the estimated outlays could be made. The disappointment in Iran was great, since an American firm, Overseas Consultants, Inc., had been invited to prepare blueprints for development and act as consultants, for which they were paid $650,000.

A complete debacle was avoided by United States foreign aid, which contributed to 37 of the seven-year projects, including the Teheran water supply and the Kuhring irrigation plans. After the fall of Mossadegh in 1953, the aid organization came to the rescue of a bankrupt government with monthly contributions of $5.25 million. Over the period 1951–April 1956, United States help in all categories amounted to $400 million.[8]

Second Seven Year Plan, 1955–62

The second Plan, focused largely on big dams and irrigation in the agricultural sector and on transport and communications, paid relatively scant attention to industry, as shown in the allocation of expenditures. Unlike the first Plan, this plan succeeded in making expenditures nearly as large as planned (95 percent), despite the fact that its last two years fell into the depression of 1960–64. In accord with the agreement of October 1954, 60 percent of the Iranian government's oil revenue during the first four years was allocated to development and, for the next three years, 75 to 80 percent. The casual nature of this Plan is indicated by the fact that it made "no claim to comprehensiveness or clarity of targets being embodied in a set of interrelated projects." [9]

Among the objectives of the second Plan was the sponsoring of investments in sugar, textiles, and cement, but two of its most prized projects fell victim to mishaps. The first of these, a proposal for an integrated iron and steel plant, would have been the second largest single investment in Iran, aside from Reza Shah's Trans-Iranian railway, and would have cost $150 million. Complications developed with the consortium of German steel plant suppliers, and the World Bank, before helping with the financing, required a preliminary survey of experts. Iran chose the Kaiser Engineers and Constructors of California, whose verdict was adverse to the large inte-

[8] Royal Institute of International Affairs, *op. cit.*, pp. 407–08, 412.
[9] *Iranian-American Economic Survey, 1967* (New York: Manhattan Publishing Co., n.d.), p. 31; hereafter referred to as *Manhattan Survey*.

Planned and Actual Expenditures of the Second Plan

	Planned		Actual
	in percent	in billion rials	in billion rials
Agriculture and irrigation	21.7	18.9	17.4
Transport and communications	34.8	30.4	27.3
Industries and mines	7.7	6.7	7.0
Social services	13.4	11.7	9.3
Regional development	14.0	12.2	8.6
Other	1.4	1.2	.4
Total development	93.0	81.1	70.0
Total nondevelopment	7.0	6.1	13.2
Total expenditure	100.0	87.2	83.2

Source: As in the preceding table.

grated plant, favoring instead a much more modest installation which would import steel billets and manufacture only end products. One of the chief members of the U.S. AID organization believes that Iran was spared a white elephant.[10]

The other favored project involved the use of the otherwise wasted natural gas by a chemical fertilizer plant and by a facility producing polyvinyl chloride. Of these the second was found impractical since the minimum feasible plant vastly exceeded Iran's domestic demand; and the first was contracted for, without consulting the Plan Organization, by the Ministry of Industries and Mines. The ambitious and able head of the Plan Organization, Mr. Ebtehaj, resigned; the crisis over the fertilizer plant had "put Plan Org's future behind it."

Nevertheless, during the years 1955–60—the first five of the second Seven Year Plan, before depression set in—Iran experienced a real boom. Evidently this cannot be ascribed to planning: it was in fact an accomplishment of private enterprise buoyed up by a generous supply of credit. From the beginning of the Plan in 1955 to its end in 1962, there was a large increase in such basic industries as cement (131 to 750 thousand tons), chromite (10 to 110 thousand tons), and cotton textiles (34,000 to 260,000 meters).[11]

Financial wherewithal for the private enterprise boom of the late fifties came first from two $45 million loan funds, one being administered by the Ministry of Industries and Mines. These funds originated in the revaluation of the gold reserve of Bank Melli, the government's foreign exchange and reserve bank, in consequence of the devaluation of the Iranian rial from 35 to 75 to the dollar. It is pointed out that, if the $45 million added to bank reserves by the loan fund for industry resulted in loans of two or three times this magnitude, some $90 to $135 million could go into industrial investment. A like amount, $45 million, went to a loan fund for agriculture, with comparable multiplier effects on private investments.

[10] Baldwin, *op. cit.*, p. 109.
[11] *Ibid.*, p. 104.

79

The second main source of funds for private industry was the Industrial and Mining Development Bank of Iran (IMDBI) which opened for business in October 1959, about the time the two loan funds of 1957 were being exhausted. The small equity capital of this bank, amounting to $10.4 million, constituted only an eighth of its total available resources, the rest coming from advances of the Iranian government, the International Bank, the U.S. government, and—about the equal of these three—the "managed loans" taken over from earlier government lending arrangements. Two-thirds of the IMDBI lending went to textiles and sugar; more than half the funds went to new firms.[12]

In concluding on the second Plan: Iran flourished and grew, but this was largely because of forces *outside* the Plan which activated private enterprise. The IMDBI proved to be "the most effective institution in the country for giving life to the government's announced policy of advancing industrialization through private investment."

Third Development Plan, 1962–68

The nearly incredible rapidity of Iran's economic rise can be indicated by a few statistics. While the 1949–55 Plan involved expected expenditures of $656 million, and the 1955–62 Plan $1,160 million, the third Development Plan, originally scheduled for $1,860 million was revised upward to $3,066 million. For this pushing up of planned expenditures, two factors were responsible. In the first place, oil revenues to Iran from the Consortium, beginning at $333 million in 1962/63, nearly doubled to $661 million by 1967/68. Secondly, because of this great increase of revenue, the government was able to increase the allocation to economic development from 55 to 80 percent over the five years of the Plan.

The budgeted expenditures of the third Plan appear as follows. Actual expenditures eventually amounted to 88.9 percent of estimates.

Planned Expenditures of the Third Plan
1962–68
(in thousands of dollars)

Sector	Amount	Sector	Amount
Agriculture and irrigation	$640,522	Health and sanitation	$176,470
Industries and mines	380,392	Manpower	43,137
Electric power and fuel	457,516	Urban development	98,039
Communications	784,313	Planning and statistics	20,915
Education	235,294	Housing and construction	137,254
Total			$3,006,532

Source: *Iranian-American Economic Survey*, 1967, p. 34.

First priority in the Plan was given to communications, followed by agriculture and irrigation, and third, power and fuel. But it is noteworthy that the total allocations to the human element in development—to education, health and sanitation, urban development and housing—somewhat exceed the portion going to agriculture

[12] *Ibid.*, pp. 114–20.

and greatly exceed that going to industry and mines. Contrasting with the second Plan, the 1962–68 Plan emphasized small irrigation projects, well digging, and the purchase of fertilizers, insecticides, and agricultural implements. The second phase of the land reform program was instituted in 1965.[13] Attention was also given to improvement of agricultural methods (orchards, vegetable gardening, rice yields, cotton culture) which in the aggregate could constitute a scientific revolution in this sector.

In the industrial sector, the period of the third Plan witnessed the launching of the large steel mill project, although this was not done under the Plan Organization, and the same is true of the chemical fertilizer plant. The third Plan also supported expansion of cotton textile capacity and of plants related to agriculture, such as vegetable oil, sugar, food processing, and the like, including fisheries. Indeed, a stated aim of government policy was to develop industries connected with agriculture and other natural resources.

A Stocktaking to Date

With the conclusion of the third Development Plan, we are close to the present, having arrived also at a juncture at which more recent quantitative data are not available. This affords an opportunity to look retrospectively not only at the results of the third Plan, but somewhat farther back, at least for important matters. The most aggregative economic indicator, gross national product, comes first. The increments to total GNP in real terms for the years of the third Plan after the depression, i.e., 1965–68, are amongst the highest increases in the world; also the near doubling of GNP in real terms for the decade 1958–68 is outstanding.

Gross National Product in Iran
1958–68
(in 1967 dollars)

	Unit	1958	1965	1966	1967	1968
Total GNP	mill.$	4,316	6,233	6,724	7,495	8,245
Change of total	percent	—	+13	+8	+12	+10
GNP per capita	dollars	206	254	266	285	304

Source: U.S. AID, *Economic Data Book, Near East and South Asia*, Iran, p. 2, Revision No. 280, March 1969.

These purely quantitative increases are the more impressive when considered jointly with the substantial expansion of the infrastructure (as shown in the fixed investment figures, below), and the solid gains in welfare. The increase of population lagged far behind the growth of output with the result that real per capita product increased by one-half over the decade. It will be observed that its increase amounted to $48 over the *seven* years following 1958 ($7 annually), while it amounted to $50 over the *three* years following 1965 ($16.6 annually).

In the process of Iran's rising to first place in oil production in the Middle East, the composite manufacturing-mining index rose very fast, especially during the later third Plan years, as shown in the figures below. But the performance of agriculture,

---

[13] See below, p. 90.

which for most countries is slow-moving, was quite marked. Electricity, beginning from low absolute levels, registered an enormous increase over the nine years 1958–67. While prices showed some increase from 1958 to 1965 as a consequence of the easy credit of the fifties, the stability of prices in the boom years of the sixties is phenomenal.

Economic Sectors, Investment, and Prices
1958–68

	Unit	1958	1965	1966	1967	1968
Agricultural index	1957–59 = 100	99	116	121	133	144P
Industrial index	1963 = 100	n.a.	127	143	170	190
Petroleum prod.	Mill. MT	40.9	94.1	105.4	128.8	140.5
Electricity per cap.	KWH	35	131	151	171	n.a.
Gross fixed invest.	Mill. $	692	1,063	1,176	1,424	1,570
Consumer prices	1963 = 100	78	106	106	107	108

P signifies provisional.
Source: As in preceding table.

Part of the eventual success of the third Plan in undoubtedly to be attributed to the stopping of the inflation of the late fifties, the costs of which were shared between the last years of Plan II and the early years of Plan III. These gains accrued partly in an inheritance of price stability from 1965 on. But, as one writer points out, the depression years' legacy of large amounts of private savings accumulated in the banks bespoke a confidence of Iranian capitalists in the political and economic stability of the country.[14]

Fourth Development Plan, 1968–72

This Plan, regarded within the country as the coping stone of Iran's modern history, aims at an 8 percent annual increase of GNP, with sectoral targets of 15 percent in industry, 4 in agriculture, 13 in oil, and 16 in electricity and gas. Past performance would seem to indicate that these goals are not too optimistic. A favorable aspect is the expectation of holding the increase in the service sector to 7.6 percent, a highly desirable aim in view of the tendency of some Middle East countries to hide unemployment in the services and the trend toward expanding the size of the bureaucracy.

Welfare objectives include greatly increasing educational facilities at all levels, adding 14,000 hospital beds, and the like.

General economic aims include an effort to narrow the gap between rural and urban levels of living; augmenting the share of industry exclusive of oil in GNP; conservation of water as the scarcest of Iran's natural resources; and last, the extension of electric power to include rural districts. The sectional allocations for new developments and new recurrent expenditures is shown in the accompanying table.

---

[14] Jahangir Amuzegar, "Nationalism vs. Economic Growth," *Foreign Affairs*, July 1966, p. 660, n. 6.

Planned Expenditures of the Fourth Plan
1968–72
(in thousands of dollars)

Sector	Amount	Sector	Amount
Agriculture, irrigation	$ 86,666	Health	$18,266
Mines, industry	153,733 [a]	Urban development	9,333
Power and fuel	115,333 [b]	Statistics	1,333
Transport, communications	113,733 [c]	Housing	30,666
Education	46,666	Others	30,933
Total			$6,400,000

[a] Includes $351,120 for petroleum and natural gas.
[b] Includes $646,666 for water development.
[c] Includes $271,066 for telecommunications.
Source: Economist Intelligence Unit, *op. cit.*, p. 5.

So ambitious is this Plan that, despite the anticipation of oil revenues increasing at accelerated rates, some $2 billion would have to be found in foreign loans. The aggregate planned investment for the five-year-plan period is $10.8 billion.

"The plan period," writes the Economist Intelligence Unit, "began in very favorable circumstances, with a high rate of economic growth inherited from the last year of the third plan and many major commitments for the fourth plan already fully supported by foreign finance." [15]

The Petroleum and Other Mineral Industries

Importance of Petroleum

Iran was the first country of the Middle East to exploit its oil resources, a concession having been granted to an Australian named D'Arcy in 1901, who "discovered" the liquid gold in 1908. In passing, oil flows or escaping gas in the region, probably ignited by lightning, were observed a half millennium before Christ, when the cult of Zoroaster incorporated fire into its mystical rites. [16] However, the commercial exploitation of the resource did not begin to acquire great significance until after the first world war, nor to become really impressive until after the second world war.

These facts appear in the following table, as well as the major break caused by the nationalization of oil, decreed on March 15, 1951, and put into force on May 1, 1951. Although the agreement of the foreign oil companies (the Consortium) with the government of Iran was concluded in 1954, four more years were required for production to exceed the annual output which had already been reached in 1950.

In the race for primacy in petroleum output, Iran literally came up from behind. As late as 1967, in a publication dedicated to Shah Mohammad Reza Pahlavi on the occasion of his coronation, it was pointed out with pride that Iran occupied third place in the Middle East and sixth in the world. Only two years later Iran had risen to first in the Middle East and a rough tie for third in the world, after the United States, the

[15] Economist Intelligence Unit, *op. cit.*, p. 5.
[16] Wilber, *op. cit.*, p. 221.

Crude Oil Production in Iran

(thousand barrels per day)

Year		Year		Year	
1915	8.1	1949	546.8	1960	1,053.3
1920	28.2	1950	649.3	1961	1,192.0
1925	88.5	1951	337.7	1962	1,322.6
1930	120.7	1952	227.2	1963	1,479.4
1935	152.8	1953	26.2	1964	1,700.5
1938	211.1	1954	70.4	1965	1,891.5
1942	191.0	1955	315.6	1966	2,118.6
1944	271.4	1956	520.6	1967	2,589.0
1946	392.0	1957	713.6	1968	2,824.1
1947	412.1	1958	810.1	1969	3,314.4
1948	508.6	1959	906.6	1970	3,737.4

Sources: 1915–1959: Sohrab Farahmand, *Der Wirtschaftsaufbau des Iran* (Basel: Kyklos Verlag, 1965), p. 94; 1960–1967: United Nations, *Statistical Yearbook*, 1967; 1968: U.S. AID, *Economic Data Book, Near East and South Asia*, Iran, p. 5, Revision No. 289, October 1969; 1969 and 1970: *Oil and Gas Journal*, December 29, 1969 and August 24, 1970. The 1970 figures are for the first six months of the year. (Tons converted to barrels per day.)

Soviet Union, and Venezuela. There is some prospect that this ranking will be improved in the visible future.[17]

How important is oil in the domestic economy of Iran? Oil production was credited with 10.6 percent of GNP in 1959/60, with 10 percent in 1965, and with 14.3 percent in 1967/68.[18] About 8 percent of the industrial labor force is engaged in various phases of this industry. In the national budget, oil royalties accounted for about 44 percent of government revenues in 1958 and during the five years from 1965 through 1969, for the following annual percentages: 53.3, 48.8, 48.7, 49.0, and 50.0. Thus, while the industry is a bonanza from a fiscal angle, there seems to be no tendency over recent years for the Iranian government to allow its dependence on oil revenues to increase.[19] Finally, oil amounts to nine-tenths of the value of exports from Iran. Western Europe is the chief market, but is declining relatively. In 1957, the world west of Suez took 61 percent, but by 1966 the figure had declined to 50. In 1957 Japan absorbed only 4 percent of Iranian petroleum exports, compared to 31 percent a decade later!

Iran possesses the largest known reserves of natural gas in the world, but only 7 percent of the flow of gas has been used, the balance being "flared," i.e., burned off. However, a major change has been set afoot, reputedly through the skilled negotiations of the Shah with Moscow. Included in the agreement were joint regulation of some rivers on the border, the construction of silos, and—of greatest importance—the building of a steel plant by the USSR. In return for these services, Iran is laying a pipe-

---

[17] The present section on petroleum makes extensive use of four articles in the *Iranian-American Economic Survey 1967*, as follows: Professor George Lenczowski, "The Contribution of the Oil Companies to Iranian Development," pp. 47–52; Baghir Mostofi, "Investment Opportunities in Petrochemicals in Iran," pp. 53–54; Dr. Reza Fallah, "The Petroleum Industry of Iran," pp. 59–62; and (unsigned) "Mineral Resources," pp. 77–81. Other sources will be separately noted.

[18] Statistical Bureau, Ministry of National Economy, quoted in *Economist Annual*, 1969, p. 3, and U.S. AID, *op. cit.*, Iran, p. 3, Revision No. 261, April 1968.

[19] U.S. AID, *op. cit.*, Iran, p. 9, Revision No. 288, September 1969; United Nations, *Statistical Yearbooks*.

line from the southern oilfields to the border to convey the natural gas which is to be supplied to the Soviet Union. This export was expected to start in 1970 at a rate of 600 million cubic feet per day, rising to 1,000 million by 1974.

On the basis of its wealth of oil and natural gas, Iran established the National Petro-chemical Company in 1965 as a subsidiary of its National Iranian Oil Company, and joined Allied Chemical in facilities to produce ammonia and sulphur. In 1966, the NPC launched a joint venture with Goodrich to turn out plastics, detergents, and caustic soda, and another joint venture with Amoco. Further and more complex petrochemical operations are contemplated under the fourth Development Plan with the expectation that the total yield of all undertakings of this sort will amount to $80 million annually.

It goes almost without saying that abundant supplies of petroleum and its products are available to the country for domestic consumption, making it the second largest per capita user in Asia after Japan.

Aside from its large shares in the GNP of Iran and its government's revenues, other substantial benefits, well described by Professor Lenczowski, accrue to the Iranian economy.[20] The oil companies' operating expenses make a contribution to the GNP which is additional to their royalty payments to the government. Their investments in construction, roads, repair shops, and the like initiate another stream of income. As in other oil producing countries in the Middle East, the companies have generally led the market in wage rates, to say nothing of numerous welfare undertakings, such as subsidized housing, health services, etc. Their training programs have introduced important skills into the country, not only in oil technology but also in the field of business administration. As provided by the Consortium agreement of 1954, the non-basic operations of the oil companies (those not directly concerned with the supplying and processing of oil and its products) such as medical, health, and housing services, plant and road construction, and other ancillary activities, are being transferred to the NIOC. This means that a corresponding amount of employment is transferred to Iranian management and the number of foreign nationals employed is being reduced in favor of native Iranians.

The Conduct of the Oil Industry in Iran

From the time of the first concession for the exploration of oil resources made to a British subject in 1901, the major operations in the industry were carried on under British auspices. Arrangements were worked out by the Anglo-Iranian Oil Company with the government for the payment of royalties; only once, in 1932, were operations interrupted when Reza Shah canceled the concessions, to be followed shortly, how-ever, by a 60-year renewal. The USSR made strenuous attempts through revolutionary and subversive tactics to "muscle in" on the exploitation of Iranian oil. Despite feeble resistance on the part of both the United Kingdom and the United States in the Azerbaijan crisis, the Iranian parliament unanimously refused to ratify an Iranian-Soviet agreement, and the Soviet offensive was brought to a halt.[21]

In 1951 the anti-foreign agitation of the so-called "National Front" led by Mossadegh came to a head in the assassination of the prime minister and a vote of the

---

[20] *Manhattan Survey*, pp. 47–50.

[21] See the succinct account of the recent political and economic history of Iran in the chapter (al-ready cited) in Lenczowski, *The Middle East in World Affairs, op. cit.*, chapter V, Iran.

parliament to nationalize the oil industry. The Anglo-Iranian Oil Company was forced to shut down and its payments to the government ceased. The result was a kind of deadlock between the Iranian government as sole owner of the petroleum deposits and the AIOC, backed by all the major oil companies, which refused to purchase oil from Iran or make their tanker fleets available for its transportation.

The matter went to the International Court of Justice in The Hague and to the United Nations Security Council with no resolution of the conflict. Other countries easily supplanted Iran in the supply of oil; the country itself was the chief loser. Finally it was the oil companies themselves which, joining together in a Consortium of eight chief producers, worked out with the Shah an acceptable solution embodied in a contract for 25 years, renewable for three five-year periods thereafter. For the immediate future, a 50-50 division of revenue was agreed upon, but the way was left open for negotiating even more favorable terms for the National Iranian Oil Company, and for a gradual reduction, at five-year intervals, of the area covered by the oil concessions. Precise percentage allocations of concessions were made to the several companies embraced in the "Iranian Participants, Ltd.," an international group incorporated in Holland, known since 1954 as "the Consortium." Aside from the eight major producers in this group, chiefly British and American, the NIOC, which owns the fixed assets used by the Consortium, handles the distribution of oil production in Iran, and deals with the companies outside the Consortium, has negotiated agreements with 23 other companies of French, Italian, and other national origins.

Subsequent legislation reaffirmed the government's exclusive ownership not only of oil and gas, but of all mineral deposits. Negotiations between oil companies and the Iranian government go on every year, not only with respect to the division of profits, but also as to the area to be released from Consortium exploitation and the rate of oil production. The results of the negotiations are a compromise, the usual uneasy peace reached by a bargaining process. "The Shah," it is said, "does not want a showdown with the companies that would lead to a reduction in his income and threaten the stability of his regime. The companies, for their part, are equally anxious to maintain good relations with a country that is not only the largest producer in the Middle East, but also ruled by an enlightened and efficient government."[22]

The trends have been toward reducing the concession areas and increasing the government's share to 75 percent or even more. Even though their share declines, the earnings of the oil companies tend to rise as the joint result of increased volume of oil production and a reputed reduction of costs per unit of output by one-half over the past five to ten years. This also accounts for the willingness of the Consortium to finance the oil shipping facilities at Kharg Island, a deep water export terminal 20 miles off the coast in the Gulf of Arabia, the largest such installation in the world. Nevertheless, there may be a limit to the ability and desire of the oil companies to carry on under increasingly onerous terms.

Other Minerals and Metals

By the legislation of 1951 and 1954, all subsurface resources belong to the state and fall under the general control of NIOC. However, the state operates some mines, leases others to foreign interests (e.g., to the British Rio Tinto), and leaves others to

---

[22] Cf. "More Revenues from Oil Companies," *Middle East Business Digest*, June 1969, p. 5.

Iranian private operators. The latter have been aided by government technical assistance, including the geological survey founded in 1962.

While an enumeration of existing mineral deposits is impressive, mining is still an infant industry. Apparently iron ore resources are modest, but the known deposits of minerals include coal, chromite, manganese, lead, zinc, sulphur, arsenic, gold, antimony, borax barytes, gypsum, and salt; recent discoveries of copper are characterized as "spectacular." Statistical evidence of the contribution of mining to the GNP is hidden, being merged with oil refining in the national accounts. While noteworthy increases in physical output in these various metals and minerals are known to have been achieved in the decade of the sixties, less than 1 percent of the labor force was engaged in the mining sector in 1966.

Agriculture

Importance and Products

Despite its unrivaled position as the largest of Middle East oil producers, Iran derives a still larger proportion of its GNP from agriculture. That proportion stood at 34.3 percent in 1959/60 but declined to 23.5 percent in 1967/68—although the absolute product of agriculture rose quite satisfactorily over the interval—because both industry and oil increased their proportions.[23] The significance of agriculture is further revealed in the composition of the labor force, 50 percent of which is in farming and farm-product processing, providing sustenance to 80 percent of the population or more, and accounting for three-fourths of all non-oil exports.

Aside from its importance on a cross-section view, the 3 to 4 percent yearly increase in value of agricultural output has contributed 1 to 2 percent to the annual 9 percent growth of Iran's national income. It has helped to increase exports, provide supplies to domestic industries, and permit a rise in the standard of living by an increase of per capita agricultural production from an index of 99 in 1958 to 108 in 1968 (1957–59 = 100).[24]

The principal food crop of Iran is wheat, which accounts for one-third of farm cash income, a culture carried on most successfully in Azerbaijan, the nation's bread basket, and more speculatively by dry farming in the northern and western parts of the country. Barley comes next in importance, and rice—cultivated chiefly along the Caspian coast—has risen to third place by virtue of a doubling of the crop over the past decade through improved seed, fertilizer, and cultivation. Other crops, including cotton, tobacco, and sugar beets, bring the proportion of field crops in total agricultural output to 45 percent. But a fortunate diversity of products is reflected in the contribution of 19 percent to total values produced by orchards and gardens (fresh and dried fruits, nuts, and vegetables), and 36 percent by livestock, milk alone constituting 21 percent.

Not surprisingly, Iran is food self-sufficient except for tea, sugar, and vegetable oils. The country's insatiable demand for tea absorbed not only the 59,000 metric tons produced domestically in 1966/67, for example, but a considerable amount im-

[23] Data regarding Iranian agriculture have been drawn from the following sources: *Economist Annual*, 1969, pp. 3–5; *Manhattan Survey*, pp. 69–74; Farahmand, *Wirtschaftsaufbau*, *passim*; and Baldwin, *op. cit*, pp 70–98, except as otherwise noted.

[24] U.S. AID, *op. cit.*, Iran, p. 5, Revision No. 289, October 1969.

ported in addition. As for agricultural exports, the highest ratios of exports to domestic markets are to be found with ginned cotton, raisins, and pistachio nuts. So far as concerns diversification, Iran has little to wish for in its agriculture.

Methods of Cultivation and Productivity

The favorable picture of Iranian farming in the aspects just treated does not hold for efficiency. First we must consider land utilization. Only 13 percent of the land area is arable, and of that, only one-third (or 16.8 million acres) is actively cropped while two-thirds (or 35 million acres) lies fallow. The amount of land actually cultivated could be expanded by greater amounts of irrigation; hence it has been said that it is not land which is in short supply, but water. However, this statement is superficial since it is said on equally good authority that, until recently, only 75 percent of the available water supply has been used. Hence the shortage of capital for irrigation purposes; or—if the oil revenues seem to provide a case of "money not a consideration" —of inefficient use of capital. But there are other inefficiencies which may be of even more immediate concern and more amenable to reform.

Of these, the most widely prevalent and intractable is traditionalism. "On the majority of farms in Iran . . . the plowing, sowing and reaping is still done by methods in use for millennia. Plowing in most areas is done by wooden plow, with iron shod plowshare, drawn by a team of oxen. Sowing is done by hand and harvesting, threshing and willowing [sic., read "winnowing"] of grain is done almost entirely by hand or with animals." [25] The use of fertilizer is a relatively recent innovation, animal dung being used, according to a nearly universal custom of the Middle East, as household fuel. At present one government fertilizer plant near Shiraz produces urea and ammonium nitrate from waste gases piped from nearby oilfields. A joint venture of the American Allied Chemicals and the Iranian National Petrochemical Company is the construction of a $170 million agricultural chemical plant at Bandar Shahpur.

Aside from irrigation projects and land reform, the principal other promising channels of improvement are education and training, mechanization, and the perfection of techniques. Beginning in 1951, the U.S. AID mission has supported 30 or more agricultural projects concerned with training and demonstration, expert assistance with pest and disease control in livestock, ground water conservation, and the like. In cooperation with the Near East Foundation, Ford Foundation, and the Point Four Organization, the Iranian plan authorities have, since 1949, spent $500,000 toward improving village schools. The government has planned 13 agricultural technical schools, which—by the termination of the third Plan—were to have educated 2,300 agricultural teachers. [26]

In Iran, the mechanization of agriculture has not been viewed with the great enthusiasm which caused some 40,000 tractors to be imported into Turkey under the Marshall Plan. For one thing, the average size of farm at 2–3 hectares (6⅔ to 10 acres) limits the applicability of machines. Another restraining consideration is the fear that mechanization might increase rural unemployment. In consequence the Third Plan did not favor the granting of credit for extending rural mechanization, but instead recommended that funds be used for simple agricultural implements, improve-

---

[25] *Manhattan Survey*, p. 70.
[26] Farahmand, *op. cit.*, pp. 46–48.

ments in breeds of stock and seeds, and the control of plant pests.[27] But an agreement has been struck with Rumania to import 3,000 tractors annually, and an assembly and later a manufacturing plant are planned for completion in 1975 to turn out 10,000 tractors per annum.

Irrigation

Aside from the well-known methods of irrigation through pumping up ground water and through ditches bringing water by gravity from streams and reservoirs, Iranian farmers from time immemorial have utilized the unique and ingenious system of *qanats*. A vertical shaft is sunk at the base of a mountain to a depth sufficient to penetrate a stratum of rock which carries down the water released by melting snows at higher altitudes. At the same time a tunnel a few feet underground is begun at the distant village, aimed toward the shaft but following contour lines to conduct its water by gravity at a sufficient but not too violent velocity. At the village the emerging water may first turn a mill and then be distributed by open ditches to the fields. Qanats frequently run for 15 or 20 miles, and occasionally reach 50. The construction and maintenance of the system absorbs a large amount of rural labor. With the recent availability of oil and power-driven pumps, the qanat system will probably decline, having given good service since the time of Darius the Great (522–486 B.C.).

In 1955 the government of Iran, under a stimulus coming from the Shah and a Dr. Ebtehaj, managing director of Plan Organization, entered into a contract for a TVA-type of project in Khuzestan with Development and Resources, Inc., of New York, represented by David E. Lilienthal and Gordon R. Clapp. The largest single component of this far-reaching project has been the Muhammad Reza Shah Pahlavi Dam on the Dez River, which will eventually bring 360,000 acres under irrigation. This project was typical of the second Plan (1955–62), which emphasized the construction of large dams and irrigation. During the course of this Plan, however, the view was urged by economists connected with the U.S. AID and other organizations that, while these gigantic projects would yield substantial benefits, they were not prospectively the best utilization of funds on a careful cost-benefit analysis. Consequently in the third Development Plan (1962–68) the emphasis was shifted to small irrigation projects, and the aid to agriculture was broadened to include the purchase of fertilizers, insecticides, and agricultural machinery and implements.

Under a plan proposed by the Shah in 1967, all water resources are eventually to be nationalized. Water resource surveys are being conducted in some regions. Agreements have been made with Russia for the joint development of rivers along the frontier, and the Aras Dam in Azerbaijan was approaching completion.

Land Tenure and Land Reform

As in nearly all Middle East countries, the distribution of land ownership in Iran prior to the reform measures of the past decade was extremely unequal, and the standard of living of the typical tenant farmer scarcely more than subsistence. Lacking reliable statistical information, estimates of the rural population who owned land run from 20 percent to a mere 5 percent. The traditional elements of production were five—

---

[27] *Ibid.*, pp. 39–46.

land, water, seed, draft animals and equipment, and labor. Under the prevalent share-cropping arrangements, the landlord furnished the land and water and took two-fifths of the product. Absenteeism on the part of landlords reduced efficiency, and the impairment of incentive was further aggravated by a custom of rotating peasants on the cultivated plots of ground.

The original impulse toward betterment of the lot of the rural population came in 1950 from the Shah himself, then 30 years of age, in a decision to distribute the crown lands. Although these lands were not actually given away as sometimes said, the Shah established a bank to make loans to the cultivators of the new land. It was apparently his hope that the large landowners would follow his example in sharply reducing their holdings.

Nothing of the sort occurred, and for more than a decade land reform fell into desuetude. In 1962, when the parliament had been suspended pending new elections and when consequently a land reform bill could not be blocked by the powerful land-owners, an ambitious and public-spirited minister of agriculture, Dr. Hassan Arsanjani, secured the approval of such a law. By its terms, landlords were permitted to own only one village, though they were allowed 40 days in which to choose which one.[28] Peasants were to remain on the land they had cultivated and were required to join cooperatives which assumed the functions of landlords. A 15-year period was provided in which they should amortize the mortgage on the land. Compensation to former landowners is said to have been less than 25 percent of the market value of the land.

Acting under this law, the minister of agriculture vigorously launched the distribution of lands held in excess of the permitted limit, despite numerous cases of resistance which cost the lives of scores of citizens and soldiers. By April 1963, when Arsanjani resigned, the government had taken possession of 2 million acres of land. Over the two years 1962-64, known as the first phase of the land reform characterized by the one-village limit, 12,875 villages had been purchased and the land sold to nearly a half million families with 2,315,950 members.

A second phase, initiated by a law of May 1964, abolished the traditional ratio of the crop-sharing formula and increased the government payment to the smaller landlords. By the time this phase ended in January 1967 with the completion of land distributions, the number of beneficiaries had been extended by over a million tenants.

Finally a third phase announced in 1967 provided for the creation of rural joint stock companies to merge the management of lands belonging to cooperating peasants. Furthermore *all* peasants leasing land from landlords were made owners, against payments spread over ten years. The law also fostered the creation of Iranian and foreign corporations to make use of lands recently made arable through the new dams and irrigation facilities.

Land in the economist's sense of the word also includes forests and fisheries, both of them valuable resources in the Iranian economy. The Caspian hardwood forests, described as "magnificent," are unique in the Middle East, despite some damage by charcoal burning and improper cutting. To protect this valuable resource, a decree supported by a popular referendum in January 1963 nationalized forests and forest pastures against compensation to former owners. The Caspian fisheries, which had

---

[28] Land titles were regarded as too vague to permit the stipulation of maximum land holding in terms of hectares or other area measure. Hence the use of "village" as a unit of measure.

been in Russian hands, were taken over in 1953 and operated by state companies. Aside from the yield in fish consumed within the country, this resource includes caviar, mostly exported and constituting a large portion of the world supply.

Planning and Agricultural Development

In the halcyon days of Iraq's economic development (1953–58), government investment was largely the result of decisions in the planning authority. Nothing of the sort could be said for Iran. The first Plan was largely abortive; during the years of the second Plan (1956–62), the building of TVA power-irrigation works did not reflect the advice of technically qualified planners; and the third Plan (1962–68), while incorporating points which the planners would not have opposed, did not result from their recommendations. "Nobody," an important foreign adviser wrote, "reads the Third Plan for Agriculture as an account of the important things that happened in the sector during the Third Plan." [29] But he also observed philosophically: "A serious land reform program, even a hastily devised one, may be more important to the country's agriculture (not to mention its politics and social structure) than a systematic development plan." [30] Certainly it was the "White Revolution" emanating from the Shah himself which produced the land reform measures of 1962–63 and their subsequent complements, and not the Plans or Plan Organization, which were largely ignored. In conclusion it may be observed that, while the formal plans in Iran emphasized short-run productivity increases, the actually-achieved increment of 3–4 percent annually has been only about the average in the Middle East. Perhaps greater, though more difficult to measure, gains lie in the reduction of inequality and the improvement in status for the rural population.

Manufacturing Industry, Excluding Oil

Chief Characteristics

Manufacturing industry in Iran is marked by four features: its relatively late start, the speed of its development recently, the importance of private enterprise, and finally the strong participation of foreign capital and businesses. Even today the level of advancement of industry in absolute terms is less than Egypt's or Turkey's. Only with the advent of large oil income around 1954 did Iran experience the beginning of an industrial revolution. But from 1959/60 to 1967/68 manufacturing rose from 8.7 to 14.4 percent of GNP; from 1963, the index of industrial production went from 100 to 190 in 1968, that is, nearly doubling. Employment in industry absorbs 10 percent of the manpower, compared to 55 percent in agriculture. Iranian manufacturing goes entirely to the domestic market save for rugs, the only industrial export, accounting, however, for one-fifth of the total export value. [31]

---

[29] Baldwin, *op. cit.*, p. 70.

[30] *Ibid.*, p. 98.

[31] Data concerning industry drawn from the following sources: *Economist Annual*, 1969, pp. 14-15; *Manhattan Survey*, pp. 23-28, 83-87, 105; U.S. AID, *op. cit.*, Iran, *passim*; Baldwin, *op. cit.*, pp. 99-139.

Historical Retrospect

The introduction of modern factories into Iran is generally credited to Reza Shah during the period 1925 to 1940. Profits from government monopolies, including those in exporting and importing, were ploughed into plants for textiles, sugar, and cement, the three most prominent industrial fields even today. Up to 1946, the beginning of the first Plan, 34 industrial and mining establishments were put into operation by the government, and 39 tea factories and rice mills. George Baldwin points out, however, that the number of these ventures is more impressive than their rentability, and that since 1956 most of them have been reorganized or sold off.

It was during the fifties that the private sector, stimulated by easy credit under the Ministry of Industries and Mines, experienced a phenomenal growth with industrial investment mounting from $60 million annually in 1956 to $120 million in 1960. During the course of the second Plan (1956–62), the emphasis of government investment was likewise put upon the construction of plants; by the conclusion of this Plan, the government owned four large integrated textile mills and two cement plants.

The second Plan also incorporated projects for a huge integrated steel mill and for two petrochemical plants, none of which were actually realized. In 1957 a German consortium made proposals for the steel mill, but they were rejected because of justifiable suspicions of their economic merit. Iran would have required foreign financing for a $150 million steel plant, and, turning to the World Bank, was advised to hire an expert team of consultants. For this role, the Kaiser Engineers and Constructors of California were engaged in 1961. Their recommendation rejected the idea of an integrated steel mill and favored only a modest beginning with a rolling mill using imported iron and steel. For the time being, this threw a wet blanket upon the Iranian aspirations.

Also under the second Plan, the Plan Organization projected two plants which should utilize the natural gas of the Iranian oil fields, otherwise going to waste, to produce petrochemicals. The first, a chemical fertilizer plant, was designed for an outlay of about $23 million by a group of Belgian consultants. The other, to cost $10 million, was proposed by Americans called Development and Redevelopment, Inc., to manufacture polyvinyl chloride (PVC) from which plastic products can be made. The fertilizer project of the Plan Organization was undercut by the Ministry of Industries and Mines, which in 1959 independently signed a contract with these three European firms to build a large nitrogen fertilizer plant. The second project, PVC, succumbed to a shortage of Plan funds coupled with misgivings concerning the adequacy of the Iranian market for even the smallest plant of this sort which could be designed. The demise of these two projects also spelled the end of the Plan Organization for the time being.

In 1965 the Iranian government contracted with the Soviet Union for a 500–600 ton annual capacity steel mill and a machine tool plant supported by a $300 million loan from the USSR to be completed by 1971. Linked with this project was a further agreement for the laying of a 750-mile gas pipeline from the southern oilfields of Iran to Astara on the Soviet border. The pipe was manufactured from imported sheet steel by two pipe mills in Ahwaz, one of them built by United States interests, having been commissioned in 1967.

The Sources of Finance for Industry

Domestic Sources

The Iranian constitution envisaged the creation of a state bank, but it was not until 1927 that the *Bank Melli Iran* (National Bank of Iran) was established. By 1940 this bank held 55,132 savings accounts with a value of $1,165,000, but in 1957—30 years after its founding—the accounts had grown to 1,109,411 in number with a value of $51,033,000. In 1957 likewise, the bank possessed some 222 branches.[32] In Teheran, one out of every four persons had a savings account. During the thirties and forties, a number of specialized state banks were created—for agriculture, mortgages, planned ventures, commerce, insurance, exports, etc. Thus, when the country came into its period of rapid growth in the fifties, it already possessed a fairly sophisticated banking organization which gathered together substantial savings from private persons and firms.

One of the first large-scale expansions of industrial credit came in 1956 when the parliament decided to utilize the increase of the monetary reserves of Bank Melli, accruing in terms of rials from the formal devaluation of that currency in 1955 from 32 to 75 to the dollar, for purposes of economic development. Agriculture and industry each received an allocation of $45 million. Assuming that this sum could support two or three times its magnitude in investments, some $90 million to $135 million, according to Baldwin's estimates, could go into industrial investment, amounting to 25–30 percent of private investment through the four to five years when it was being disbursed. Two-thirds of the total was allocated as loans to textiles and sugar, two industries which were already the largest in the country.

The second measure taken by the government on behalf of industry was the founding of the Industrial Mining and Development Bank of Iran (IMDBI) in 1959. The bank, however, was in fact a private institution, since its share capital was subscribed in about equal amounts by Iranian and foreign individuals and firms. Beside the equity capital, some seven-eighths of its capital of $42.4 million came from outside loans, of which half originated in the loan portfolio of earlier government industrial funds and one-half from loans by the Iranian government, the International Bank, and the United States government.

Some indication of the success of this institution is afforded by its increasing dividends to shareholders, in successive years after its creation, of 4, 6, 6½, 7, and 8 percent plus a 20 percent stock dividend, while interest charged on its loans was lowered from 10 to 9 and finally to 8 percent. Small wonder that the IMDBI has been called "the most effective institution in the country for giving life to the government's announced policy of advancing industrialization through private investment." [33] Further tributes to the viability of this institution were additional loans made to it by the International Bank of $10 million in 1965, $25 million in 1966, $25 million in 1968, and $40 million in 1969.[34]

Foreign Sources

In 1955 a law was passed entitled Law for the Attraction and Protection of Foreign Capital. It guaranteed the safety of foreign investments made in Iran and ensured

---

[32] Wilber, *op. cit.*, pp. 264-65.
[33] Baldwin, *op. cit.*, p. 119.
[34] *Economist Annual*, 1969, p. 15.

repatriation for both capital and interest. In addition, foreign investors were granted generous tax holidays and the enjoyment of all advantages accorded to domestic investors. The Iranian-American Economic Survey of 1967 gives the names, addresses, and types of business of 100 American firms operating in Iran.[35] The list includes Caterpillar Tractor, Eastman Kodak, General Electric, Gillette, IBM, Lockheed, Merck, National Cash Register, Parke-Davis, Singer, Westinghouse, etc., but excludes the oil companies. Scores of companies from other countries have taken advantage of the 1955 law. In most cases, it is said, these companies have gone into partnerships with Iranians for the sake of their knowledge of Iran customs, laws, and economic conditions, including relations with labor and the government. The predominant field for foreign investors is industry.

The contributions of United States AID to Iran over the years 1946 to 1968 amount to $1,923.1 million in economic and military aid, a sum exceeded in the Middle East only by Greece and Turkey.[36] In addition, private American assistance in the fields of education, sanitation, and rural development has been given over a period of 20 years by the Near East Foundation. Technical assistance and business management methods have been supplied by the International Executive Service Corps since 1965 through its arranging and financing sojourns of American business executives with Iranian firms, as well as technical experts' production techniques. Such activities make substantial contributions to what has come to be called "personal capital," i.e., the skills and knowledge of individuals as productive agents.

Other Economic Aspects

The center of the moving spectacle of economic development in Iran is, of course, occupied by the oil industry, by industry in general, and by agriculture—less for its rate of increase than for its very creditable performance relative to this sector in other developing countries, and for its widespread human benefits. But the three leading sectors named typically do not account for more than half the GNP of Iran. The "other economic aspects" are, in the aggregate, equally important; and without their support, however lacking in dramatic quality, the main sectors could not have made their outstanding records.

Electrical Power

Iran possesses ample resources in oil and water power for its foreseeable demand for electrical power. After a preliminary survey, a loan of $6.5 million was made in 1966 by United States AID to support the work of a newly established Ministry of Water and Power. A master plan is being implemented by the Iran Electrical Administration for an integrated national power grid, in which the World Bank participates. For the larger population centers, such as Teheran, Isfahan, and Shiraz, natural gas will be used for generations; for smaller localities, oil will be employed. Thus for future expansion, hydroelectric energy will be a by-product only of water supply for irrigation, and for municipal and industrial use. Electricity rose from an index of 54.0 (1962/63 = 100) in 1959/60 to 193.0 in 1966/67.

---

[35] Iranian-American Economic Survey, 1967, pp. 151–62.
[36] See table in the Appendix.

Transport and Communications

It is worthy of note that in the first three Development Plans, transport and communications received a larger planned allocation of funds than any other sector of the economy.[37] Even in the present (or fourth) Plan, this sector receives an allocation which is second only to industry, at 100.3 billion rials compared to 125.3 billion rials, and compared to 480.0 billion rials for all sectors.[38] This strong emphasis upon the transport sector is explained by a glance at the map which will reveal Iran as the largest country in area, aside from Saudi Arabia, in the Middle East. Even after several decades of investment in this sector, Iran had in 1966 only 21 miles of improved roads per 1,000 square miles, compared to 95 in Turkey, 40 in Iraq, and—at the end of the list—five in Yemen.[39]

In other respects, the transportation situation is better. The railway system, given its great impetus by Reza Shah's construction of the 850-mile Trans-Iranian line, now has a total length of 2,300 miles. Under the CENTO organization, a rail connection is being established with Turkey. With World Bank help important improvements have been made in the highway system, and the Export-Import Bank has contributed to the maintenance of the roads. Airlines, ocean shipping, and ports have also been greatly expanded.

Money, Banking, and Prices

After the one-time pattern of many less-developed countries, the Bank Melli Iran, established in 1927, served for more than three decades in a combined capacity of bank of issue, government depository, foreign exchange authority, and commercial bank. In 1960, its central banking functions were transferred to a new institution, the Central Bank of Iran, while Bank Melli continued as a government commercial bank. There are nine other state or joint state-private banks designed for special functions, such as industry, agriculture, and the like. Foreign banking activity is permitted only as joint ventures with Iranian banks.

Perhaps the most striking feature of the monetary situation has been that during the years of great expansion, 1965-68, the index of wholesale prices dropped from 114 (1958=100) to 107, and the cost of living fell from 132 to 108. This is a record without parallel among developing countries. The Iranian rial, understandably, has of late maintained parity with Western currencies.

Public Finances

Until July 1964, the Iranian budget was an extremely complex matter, with numerous special budgets and funds for various boards, departments, state industries, and the like. After the reorganization, the budget was indeed simplified, but redefinitions and reclassifications make it impossible to compare budgets before and after the revision. Furthermore, while the deficits have not been hidden, information is not published as to the proportions of the deficits covered by domestic versus foreign borrowing, nor as to the amount and source of foreign grants and loans. Those emanating from the United States are published by AID and are included in the following table.

---

[37] Cf. pp. 78, 79, and 80 above.
[38] *Economist Annual* 1969, p. 5.
[39] U.S. AID, *Economic Data Book, Near East and South Asia*, Table 1, Revision No. 277, December 1968.

Iran: Central Government Finances
(in billions of rials)

	1965	1966	1967	1968	1969
Total Revenues	95.2	97.3	110.2	132.1	160.6[a]
Expenditures, total	99.9	108.8	140.3	179.2	204.8[a]
of which: defense	22.2	24.4	33.3	(41.9)	49.1
Deficit (−)	−4.7	−11.5	−30.1	−43.0	−44.2
Official loans & grants	1.0	7.3	10.1	26.4	n.a.
U.S. AID, total [b]	6.8	8.6	13.7	9.6	n.a.
of which: economic [b]	3.2	1.6	8.0	3.2	n.a.

[a] Budget basis.   [b] Converted from dollars at 75 rial = $1.

Source: U.S. AID, *Economic Data Book, Near East and South Asia*, Iran, p. 5, Revision 289, October 1969.

With regard to military expenditures, an international comparison made recently by Professor Hoffmann of Munster reveals that in 1966 Iran devoted to this purpose the *lowest proportion of GNP* among 58 countries, at 0.38 percent. Among 59 countries, its military outlays absorbed a below-average *share of public expenditures* at 23 percent, lying between the 0–5 percent group of six small nations and the three highest— the United States with 42, Turkey with 54, and Burma with 65 percent. Finally, on a *dollars per capita* expenditure for military purposes, Iran occupied a modest position at $9.67 in 1966, with 19 other nations between $5–$25. This was higher than the lowest group of 20 nations, between $0–$5, but far below the highest group of four which exceed $100.[40]

With regard to budget deficit, it has not always been covered by the reported total of foreign grants and loans, a fact which implies an increase of domestic borrowing or money issue. So far as concerns money issue, the increase of the index (1963 = 100) from 126 in 1965 to 187 in 1969 can scarcely be regarded as excessive when real GNP was increasing by 9 or 10 percent annually, a judgment reinforced by the concomitant fall in prices. Recent figures of domestic and foreign debt are not available, but the judgment of foreign creditors has proved quite favorable to Iran. Loan repayments of $91 million, fully maintaining the service of the debt, amounted to only one-fourth of the favorable trade balance of $361 million in 1968.

Foreign Trade and Balance of Payments

To no one's surprise, all items of Iran's exports shrink into insignificance relative to oil. This fact is at once favorable and fatal— favorable as the basis of Iran's present-day affluence, fatal in the great dependence of the nation on the vicissitudes of one source of wealth and income.

---

[40] Walter G. Hoffmann, "Der Anteil der Verteidigungsausgaben am Bruttosozialprodukt—Ein internationaler und intertemporaler Vergleich," *Kyklos*, XXIII, 1970, Fasc. 1.

Iran's Chief Exports
(in millions of dollars)

	1958	1965	1966	1967	1968
Oil	625[a]	1,136	1,147	1,749	1,686
Cotton	15[b]	39	39	38[b]	42[b]
Fruits and nuts	21[b]	23	20	17[b]	28[b]
Carpets	17[b]	46	38	41[b]	59[b]

[a] It is a somewhat amusing fact that the figures on oil are based on the Western year, beginning January 1, while [b] the others are usually based on the solar (fiscal) year beginning March 21.

Source: U.S. AID, *Economic Data Book, Near East and South Asia*, Iran, p. 6, Revision No. 289, October 1969.

The distribution of main imports is shown in the following figures. For imports, the optimistic aspect is that these chief imports are typical development goods, which take the place of the wasting asset, petroleum; on the other side, the absolute and increasing size of imports has been a matter of concern to the Iranian authorities.

Iran's Chief Imports
(in millions of dollars)

	1958	1965	1966	1967	1968
Machinery and transport equipment	90[a]	306	362	703[a]	537[a]
Iron and steel	51[a]	133	145	242[a]	207[a]
Chemicals	24[a]	102	118	109[a]	115[a]

[a] Figures for fiscal year beginning March 21.
Source: As for preceding table.

On the export side of Iranian foreign trade, a striking fact is the rapid rise of Japan, now the third largest industrial nation, and by virtue of this the largest purchaser of Iranian oil in Asia. Oil exports also account for the positions of the United Kingdom and India. Since the United States does not itself take much Middle East oil, its purchases from Iran have to fall into that country's less important export categories.

Because Iran's imports are largely development capital goods, it is not surprising that they come from the world's leading industrial countries. Germany now leads the list, probably on the result of aggressive salesmanship, price competition, and traditional ties with Iran.

In 1964, Iran, Turkey, and Pakistan established the Regional Cooperation for Development (RCD), devoted to integrating the economic development of these three nations and furthering cultural exchange. After five years, this effort can register some successes, such as the joint establishment of eight varied industrial projects now in actual operation, and nine more joint ventures in process of elaboration. Various research studies have been made, some accompanied by conferences and projects for appropriate policies, in the fields of mutual trade, banking, insurance, tourism, transportation, and technical cooperation. A Regional Cultural Institute has been

Chief Trading Partners of Iran

	1958	1965	1966	1967	1969
Exports (f.o.b., in millions of dollars)					
Japan	35	206	269	533	577
United Kingdom	157	160	186	431	322
India	69	69	39	74	112
United States	42	69	83	66	75
Communist bloc	29	39	38	56	61
Imports (c.i.f., in million dollars)					
Germany	62	170	205	243	311
United States	72	155	172	209	239
United Kingdom	55	111	117	140	161
Japan	39	67	74	77	123
Communist bloc	57	39	71	81	106

Source: As in the preceding tables.

established in Teheran with branches in Istanbul, Lahore, and Dacca, and the exchange of students and the publication of regional studies progress. RCD is said to have entered extensively into the large area of regional development. [41]

Beside the RCD, Iran participates in agreements with the European Economic Community and it has entered bilateral trade and payments agreements with the Soviet government and all the Communist neighbors on the western periphery of the USSR.

For a bird's-eye view of the international financial situation of Iran in recent years, we turn to the balance of payments and its principal components. Lines 1–6 show the evolution of the current account, lines 7–12 show the capital account. Since minor items, together with "errors and omissions," have been omitted, the table does not show a complete balance. It can be seen that, despite the large and increasing magnitude of Iran's exports (line 2), which include oil revenues and the outlays in foreign exchange of the oil companies, and despite the fact that Iran's visible imports (line 3) are less than her visible exports by the amounts on line 4, the *invisible imports* (line 5) are sufficiently large to produce deficits in the balance on current account (line 1) from 1965 on. The chief explanation of the large invisible import figure *and* of the current account deficit is given by line 6, payments of interest and profits to foreign investors.

---

[41] "RCD: 5 Years of Progress," *Middle East Business Digest*, June 1969, pp. 6–9.

Principal Items in the Balance of Payments of Iran
(in millions of dollars)

Items	1964	1965	1966	1967	1968 P
1. Balance on goods and services	33	−107	−131	−137	−340
2. Exports, f.o.b.	1,137	1,253	1,392	1,662	1,860
3. Imports, c.i.f.	−661	−873	−964	−1,181	−1,499
4. Trade balance ("visibles")	476	380	428	481	361
5. Total services ("invisibles")	−443	−487	−559	−618	−701
6. of which: payments on foreign investments	−362	−397	−448	−553	−641
Capital movements					
7. Private direct investments	6	234	80	35 } → 60	
8. Other private long term	1	5	6	12 }	
9. Government receipts of loans and credits	6	75	129	175	441
10. of which: U.S. loans	5	46	84	86	n.a.
11. Government repayments on loans	−67	−70	−40	−47	−91
12. Reserves of central banks	52	−62	−9	−55	104

P signifies preliminary figures for the year.
Source: International Monetary Fund.

To add one interesting detail not shown in the table: for the ratio of Iran's "other" exports (*visible and invisible*, beside oil) to the total of oil revenues *plus* oil company outlays in foreign exchange, during the fiscal years 1964/65 to 1968/69, the figures are 17.5, 32.3, 46.4, and 36.6 percent. These ratios serve to correct the somewhat exaggerated importance of oil which comes from looking at oil *exports* instead of foreign oil companies' *payments* (revenue paid to government plus purchases of rials), which are only about half as large as oil exports.

The first three lines of the capital account (lines 7, 8, and 9) explain how Iran can run the adverse balance on current account shown in line 1. It is a common characteristic of developing countries to draw upon foreign private and foreign capital to pay for the capital goods which are so essential a source of economic growth. Hence it is not debt per se but excessive debt which is dangerous, excessive being defined as an amount which imposes an undesirable burden on the export capacity of the country or so large as to alarm foreign creditors. Unlike Turkey, Iran has not—except for the oil crisis years—had difficulties in maintaining the service of its foreign debt; and unlike Egypt, it has not allowed foreign debt to rise while taking large imports of foodstuffs.

But to render a final judgment on this question, one would have to know the absolute size of the foreign debt, and these figures have not been published in recent years. Evidently the Iranian government has felt somewhat uncomfortable concerning its deficit on current account. In its annual negotiations with the Consortium oil companies, it tries very hard to increase the Iranian share of their profits; furthermore, it has limited imports through tariffs and quotas and promoted exports by various incentives. But on the whole, the balance-of-payments deficit does not present itself as one of Iran's chief problems.

For a quarter of a century, Iran's balance of payments, the economic growth of the country and its political security have been substantially strengthened by U.S. foreign aid. From 1946 through 1968, Iran received about $1.2 billion in military aid, compared to Turkey's $3.0 billion and Greece's $2.0 billion, all of these far in excess of other Middle East countries. In economic aid, amounting to $770 million, it received less than Israel and the United Arab Republic and far less than Turkey and Greece, all four of these being non-oil countries.[42]

Welfare

The most general indicator of economic welfare is per capita real income. Over the decade 1958–69, Iran scored an enviable record, for—despite the second highest rate of population increase in the Middle East at 3.2 percent per annum—the absolute increment of GNP was sufficient to raise per capita income in real terms from $206 to $304. At the same time, literacy, education, and health improved, and—while no satisfactory statistics exist to measure it—the distribution of wealth and income has become more equal.

Because 85 to 90 percent of the population is rural, the most pervasive influence in all these respects has been the land reforms initiated by the Shah early in his reign and carried forward in his White Revolution program launched on January 23, 1963 as a six-point program, subsequently expanded to nine and finally to 12 points.[43] The strictly agricultural aspects have been set forth; but it is worth repeating that some of the most beneficial features for the rural population have been the cooperative organizations and cultural technological programs which accompany the allocations of land. Amongst these—benefiting urban as well as rural populations—are the Literacy Corps and the Reconstruction and Development Corps, manned partly by young recruits during their compulsory military service.

During the first four years of its activity, the Literacy Corps sent 32,000 persons into the villages to combat the prevailing illiteracy rate of 80 to 85 percent. Some 250,000 adults and 600,000 children were taught to read and write, and 10,000 schools were built.[44] Working in conjunction with the Health Corps, likewise financed by the army through providing the first four months of the recruits' training period, sanitary teams have drilled some 4,000 wells. During the past five years, the incidence of malaria has been reduced from 90 to 3 percent.

Other parts of the White Revolution are operating successfully. A highly qualified Iranian economist and official declares that, "The profit-sharing plan, contrary to the

---

[42] Cf. the table in the Appendix, p. 119.

[43] The program is colorfully and fully described by the Shah himself; cf. Mohammed Reza Pahlavi Aryamehr, *The White Revolution* (Teheran: The Imperial Pahlavi Library, 2d ed., 1967).

[44] John Scott, *The Middle East at War*, published by *Time* magazine, 1970, pp. 11–12.

unfavorable predictions and thanks to its flexibility, has not stopped private (foreign and domestic) investments in the country." [45] The original six-point program gave women a voice in the government through new electoral laws. In 1967 the parliament passed a Family Protection bill giving women greater legal rights, particularly regarding divorce; polygamy has been virtually abolished. A private organization, the Women's Organization of Iran, dispenses information concerning family planning; it also trains urban women workers for rural community development.

Education offered and still offers a field urgently requiring reform from the lowest to the highest levels. In the rural areas, for example, 19 percent of the children at school were girls, against 40 percent in the towns and cities. The paucity of schools can readily be inferred from some figures as to the changes which could be made in the span of 12 years.

Primary and Secondary Schools in Iran

	1952	1964
Number of schools	4,152	23,931
Total enrollment	852,265	2,929,853
Enrollment of girls	2,000	941,500
Number of teachers	25,000	83,500

Source: Luanna J. Bowles, "American and Foreign Support of Education in Iran," in *Manhattan Report*, pp. 127–31.

With regard to higher education, the number of persons attending college was reported for 1965 to be 24,700 in a population of 24.55 million in that year. However, the matter for concern is less the enrollment than the quality of higher education. The University of Teheran is criticized by a qualified American observer as follows: [46]

Teheran is organized on the lines of 19th century French universities: . . .didactic instruction by lecture methods that emphasize rote learning; all-or-nothing testing through a single written examination at the end of the year; few contacts between faculty and students; little reading beyond lecture notes; and a pattern of part-time service from faculty members who tend to regard their posts as bases from which to engage in outside employments that often get the lion's share of their attention. [47]

Since 1950 American aid has been active in the field of education in Iran, providing advisers to the Ministry, assistance in teacher training, teaching materials including texts, and periods of study for Iranian educators in the United States. Vocational training for soldiers of the army was instituted by the AID Mission in 1961, in masonry, carpentry, tailoring, auto mechanics, electrical work, and welding. This program, lasting three months, produced about 7,000 graduates each year.[48]

[45] Amuzegar, *op. cit.*, p. 658.

[46] The present writer, representing the UNESCO, was chairman of a mission of three, including representatives of the Economic Commission for Latin America and the Organization of American States, to appraise the character of economic education in the universities of Latin America. The Mission found the same shortcomings in those universities as are ascribed to Teheran. Cf. *The Teaching of Economics in Latin America* (Washington, D.C.: The Pan American Union, 1961). During a year's sojourn in India, I observed some of the same difficulties.

[47] Baldwin, *op. cit.*, p. 161.

[48] *Manhattan Report*, pp. 85 and 127–32.

The labor force of Iran was estimated at 8 million in 1966, which was 31 percent of the population; of the active labor force, not more than 10 percent were women. Labor unions, with about 100,000 members, are said not to be a significant factor among Iranian workers. Actual work stoppages of any duration do not occur, the Labor Law of 1959 having laid down the procedures for settling disputes. "Working conditions and wage levels in industries covered under the Foreign Investment Law are such that few reasons have existed for disputes." [49]

The concern of government for human welfare is exemplified by its policies designed to avoid excessive concentration of population in large cities. Tax holidays have been eliminated for new manufacturing industries in Teheran, and attractive industrial parks have been established in Ahwaz and Tabriz to reduce pressure on the capital city.

In conclusion, it would be difficult to emphasize too greatly the benefits of the relative political stability of Iran for economic development and social welfare. "In direct contrast to the Iranian situation, bloody revolutions, military coups and experiments with various kinds of socialism and capitalism among Iran's neighbors to the west and southwest have failed the tests of survival or success." [50]

Retrospect and Prospect

Even including the depression years 1960–64, the economy of Iran grew at an annual rate for the decade of 1958–68 at 9 percent in real terms. This surmounted the 3.2 percent of population growth—the second highest in the Middle East—leaving a growth rate of per capita real income of 4.2 percent. International comparisons based on earlier periods such as those made for other countries of this study would understate the rapidity of Iran's development, which came at an accelerating rate during the whole of the sixties. It is safe to say that no other country in the Middle East, perhaps none elsewhere, has equaled the record of Iran from 1964 on.

If this retrospect is cause for gratification, it may be well to recall that Iran is still a poor country with a per capita real income of $304 (in 1967 dollars), not much exceeding the median for developing countries in general. Furthermore, poverty is widespread, the distribution of wealth and income grossly unequal. In assessing the future, therefore, it would be well not simply to project the immediate past, but to consider the character of the Iranian economy and the reasons for its great advance. Are there sound reasons for expecting it to continue?

Distinctive Features of the Economic Development of Iran

One significant feature is couched in the following trenchant terms by a former member of the United States AID mission: "Iran is a country where economic development is succeeding but where economic planning, as the process is usually understood, has failed." [51] This judgment gives grounds for pessimism in the mind of its author, who believes that the failure of planning is to be ascribed to the perversities of Iranian politics and important antisocial characteristics of its people. Admittedly the planning could scarcely be proved faulty; the trouble was its being very largely

---

[49] *Ibid.*, p. 86.
[50] Amuzegar, *op. cit.*, p. 657.
[51] Baldwin, *op. cit.*, p. vii.

ignored. But this has been the fate of planning rather generally in the Middle East, including even the socialist countries such as Egypt and Iraq. As the level of education and economic sophistication rises, it is quite possible that planning can be more influential, and there is no special reason for excluding Iran from this possibility.

A second distinctive characteristic of the recent economic history of Iran has been the relatively large role played by private enterprise. This has in part been due to the "emergence of a new segment of the bourgoisie with both the enterprise and the managerial capacity to run modern factories." [52] In some measure this must be owing to the examples of successful business set by the oil companies, their training programs, and their incorporation of Iranians into managerial positions. American and other private capital have played significant parts in the growth of the petrochemical industry. There are some 200 American firms in Iran operating in a great diversity of enterprises. Professor Issawi points out that American business has brought technical and managerial skills into Iran and an entry into world markets. Thus far the country has not developed a xenophobic passion for "Iranization," fortunately for its economic future. Indeed, even the word has an unreal sound. Finally, industrialization through private enterprise has been an announced policy of the government, and it has been implemented by generous supplies of credit.

Thirdly, the recent history of Iran has shown a remarkably strong concern for human welfare. In considerable degree this must be ascribable to the Shah's Six Point Program of 1963, but it was evident in the earlier measures of land distribution. Only in Israel has there been greater government activity directed toward welfare ends, and only in Egypt has land reform made a comparable contribution to the improvement of the lot of the agricultural population. But land reform, together with its community developments and cooperative ventures, is not the only sector. The third Development Plan—as has been pointed out—involved larger allocations to human improvement, thanks to industry and agriculture together.[53] An experienced observer and world traveler observes that "Iran stands out as the country which has made the most significant economic and social progress in the Moslem Middle East. The best way to confirm this is to visit the country." [54]

Factors Underlying Iran's Rapid Development

Iran's economic success, especially since the end of the oil crisis in 1954, no doubt comes from a rare combination of favorable circumstances, some fortuitous, some meritorious. In all candor, I should be obliged to give first rank to the fortuitous presence of fabulous petroleum resources. Of course, the history of Iraq demonstrates that wealth and well-being do not necessarily follow; but the advantages to a country of having most of the costs of government defrayed by nontax revenue and of acquiring the largest part of its economic infrastructure in the same way scarcely require elaboration.

Aside from this, it is political stability which has favored Iran's development. In part this also can be ascribed to the essentially fortuitous circumstance, shared also by Turkey, of not being a part of the Arab world and hence not being automatically in-

---

[52] Issawi, "Iran's Economic Upsurge," *op. cit.*, p. 449.
[53] Cf. p. 82 above.
[54] Scott, *op. cit.*, p. 14. He also calls Iran the "Coming Power" of the Middle East.

volved in the Arab-Israeli conflict. But political stability has resulted also from the tough tactics of Reza Shah in suppressing separatist factions, and from the adroitness of Shah Mohammed Reza Pahlavi in weathering the Mossadegh regime and the Shah's demonstration of political sagacity subsequently. An essential element of that sagacity was his recognition of the necessity of economic and political improvement for the common man. Another element is that, in a setting in which the ideal of Western democracy is probably impossible of immediate achievement, the Shah's authoritarianism has been moderate. It keeps the opposition in check but gives wide latitude to personal liberty, as for example, freedom to travel and study abroad, conduct business with foreigners, and the like.

Thirdly, more successfully than other Middle East countries, Iran has steered a course between the *laissez-faire* economic and social policy of the old regime in Saudi Arabia and the top-heavy bureaucracy of the socialist United Arab Republic. Thus the nation's birthright of forests and subsurface resources had been declared public property. But, for the most part, the evolution of industry has been left to private enterprise, assisted by government in numerous ways, including finance and—where necessary— special financial incentives. The most recent indication of Iran's support of its private enterprise system was the announcement in March 1970, that the field of industrial activity would be left entirely to the private sector while industrial investments in the public sector would be restricted to the expansion of present state-owned industries.[55]

In agriculture, Iran made no unnecessary detour over collectivism, as in the Yugoslavian case, to arrive at a more democratic distribution of land ownership and a minimum of rural welfare. Iran has avoided the heavy apparatus of state monopolies, such as prevails in Turkey, preferring instead to leave the entrepreneurial burden to private owners. "A few of the government plants have proved viable, but many have not. So it is particularly significant that since World War II a vigorous private sector has emerged in response to favorable money and fiscal conditions created by government."[56] Easing the process of land reform and possibly preventing a counter-revolution, was the availability of oil revenues out of which to compensate the former landlords. And the availability of foreign financial and technical aid undoubtedly smoothed the path of private enterprise. Thus illuminated policy and good luck combined in the Iranian success story.

What of the Future?

From the angle of *Realpolitik*, as Professor Lenczowski points out, there are several powerful factors which will protect Iran from the internal disasters which have beset its neighbor Iraq. The fact that it is not an Arab nation has already provided an insulation from the Israeli issue, and this will persist in the future. In the second place, like others of the northern tier of Middle East countries such as Turkey and Pakistan, Iran has had too much experience with Soviet machinations to tolerate any serious threat to its domestic peace from the side of the extreme left. Finally, the monarchy as presently constituted portends political continuity as in no other country of the region.[57]

---

[55] *Iran News and Documents*, Ministry of Information, Teheran, Iran, Vol. I, No. 50, March 9, 1970
[56] Baldwin, *op. cit.*, p. 137.
[57] Lenczowski, *The Middle East in World Affairs, op. cit.*, p. 232.

The character of Reza Shah Pahlavi's regime conduces to future political stability from both the foreign and domestic angles, since the Shah has succeeded in maintaining or evoking the goodwill and help of both the United States and the Soviet Union, and in internal affairs has won support through his social and economic reforms. But there is, of course, the risk of assassination—as on earlier occasions—by an individual fanatic or member of a revolutionary group, with uncertain results regarding the quality of the succession.

Some observers of the Iranian scene have taken a skeptical position because of what they conceive to be the grave defects of individual conduct and unethical behavior of the population generally. This is, indeed, the main theme of one author who writes, for example:

> All outsiders agree that the Iranians are masters in their own diabolical, nonconstructive way of handling interpersonal relations. But in a society committed to the development of an ever changing, self-generating economic system, based on trust and flexibility in interpersonal relations, this kind of intellect not only is useless but also an obstacle.[58]

In like vein, another writer—for whom, however, this is only an incidental theme in a book devoted to economic subjects—observes:

> . . . no businessman can get a loan or a license, or make a sale to government, or secure a government contract or have a telephone installed, or receive payment on a bill presented, or move goods out of customs without either securing the intervention of a friend in high places or purchasing his objectives through bribery, or both." [59]

Characterizations of an entire people are notoriously subjective and unreliable. Whatever elements of truth may be present in these indictments, it is evident by most objective criteria that Iran has moved forward anyway; there seems to be no reason for not projecting the trend, recognizing the fallibility of all human judgments.

In conclusion, it seems desirable to point to two important factors. The one is demographic. A rate of population increase of 3.2 means that gross national product must increase enormously to provide a rising level of income and welfare; in the long run such a rate would be intolerable. But the very fact that Iran has supported such a rate over a number of years and still has produced a strong increase in per capita income indicates what could be achieved in a material way if the birth rate can be controlled. The political and social incentives should be powerful.

Finally, against the sinister possibility that something may happen to Iran's oil prosperity stands the fact that a high proportion of the oil revenues have gone consistently into building up the country's economic infrastructure and productive apparatus. It may well be that Iran is the "coming power" of the Middle East.

---

[58] Norman Jacobs, *The Sociology of Development—Iran as an Asian Case Study* (New York: Frederick A. Praeger, Inc., 1966), p. 265.
[59] Baldwin, *op. cit.*, p. 17.

VI. SOME INSIGHTS CONCERNING ECONOMIC DEVELOPMENT IN THE MIDDLE EAST

Five quite unlike countries of the Middle East have been surveyed for the purpose of discovering the characteristics of their development in the years since the first world war, especially during the past quarter of a century. The peculiarities of each history have inevitably absorbed attention in the particular cases; but in the final analysis, their bearing upon general conclusions is the thing of greatest interest. What is to be learned concerning the nature of economic development in the Middle East? The analysis begins with some basic, quasi-physical facts about the supply of resources, dealing thereafter with general economic systems, specific economic institutions including planning, personal endowments and behavior, the demographic factor, and political stability and instability, concluding finally with some observations on American policy.

Economic Resources

Natural Resources: Land

Let us think first of agriculture in order to offset the popular tendency to identify it with the old-fashioned and hopeless and to glorify industry as the path to progress and general welfare. Even in the Middle East with its deserts, aridity, and impoverished soils, this is an error. Some of the oil-rich nations could or do afford, on the basis of present money costs, to import much or most of their foodstuffs. But to ignore domestic agriculture would be to ignore the fact that oil is a wasting asset and one dependent upon the vagaries of international markets and politics. Even as large an oil producer as Iran has not permitted itself to fall victim to this myopia because a large proportion of its population still derives its living from the land. The arithmetic process of averaging out oil revenues over the whole population has not eliminated rural poverty and open or concealed unemployment.

In countries such as Turkey and Egypt, not as yet possessed of significant oil revenues, the case for improving agriculture is, of course, stronger. In both countries, because of the limited industrial base two decades ago, the recent rates of increase of industry have been prepossessing. Industrialization could scarcely be characterized as mistaken. But in both countries it has produced widespread complaints of bureaucratic inefficiency, lack of articulation with the economy, artificial price systems, and waste. Together with limited supplies of industrial skills and managerial talents, and with the limits to domestic markets imposed by the existing structure of wealth and income, these flaws have led qualified observers to believe that agriculture in both Egypt and Turkey must advance as a backstop to further expansion of industry. Very few industries in these or other Middle East countries give promise of going beyond the domestic markets into successful competition with the strong sources of international supply.

Natural Resources: Oil

The well-known facts about oil in the Middle East are the enormous revenues it produces for some governments, the large share of the region in world production and reserves, and the political power which oil confers in the international scene. The oil income of 13 Arab and three non-Arab countries over the past two decades runs to more than double the magnitude of the aid they have received from the United States, the Soviet bloc, and the World Bank, taken together.

The more negative side of the story may well begin with the very concept of economic development. Not uncommonly it is defined as an increase of per capita national income, a definition which is satisfied statistically by the mounting petroleum royalties. Unlike the proceeds of foreign loans or grants, which have first to be successfully invested in order to produce income, oil royalties *are* income, however it is spent.

Thus it could come about that, after more than a decade of oil income putting it into the fourth place in the Middle East, Iraq could find itself in the early sixties at a practical standstill by virtually all tests of development, indeed, even while those revenues continued to rise! Internal warfare and international strife have brought Iraq into a traumatic state from which it has not yet escaped. The moral is not that oil revenues are unimportant, but that they merely offer the *opportunity* for economic development. Because this revenue accrues virtually without effort on the part of the recipient, it is peculiarly subject to being wasted. Substantial parts of the drainage and irrigation projects realized by Iraq with its income from oil in the good years of the fifties, it is reported, have fallen into desuetude and decay during the past decade.

On the other hand, Iran affords an example of an oil producer which has been turning the wasting asset of petroleum into other types of national assets. It has made solid advances in the agricultural, industrial, and other types of economic infrastructure; and it has built up its human capital in improvements in health, education, and general welfare.

In addition to the fact that oil revenue comes from a wasting asset, it is also exposed to economic vicissitudes which exceed those of an economy resting on a broad base of industry, agriculture, and commerce. Here and now, oil generally bestows billions which bedazzle everyone; in fact, however, oil is an extreme example of the vulnerabilities of the so-called "mono-culture" economies. Iraq's decline began in 1957 with the cutting off of its outlets to the Mediterranean through the pipelines running across Syria; even Lebanon felt the interruption of its revenue from transit petroleum. Furthermore, as matters stand, no one country in the Middle East has a strong bargaining position vis-a-vis the buyer. While the tendency recently has been for the share retained by the supplying country to surpass quite considerably the 50 percent which has become conventional, this may be held in check by oil discoveries in places as far removed as Alaska, Australia, South Africa, and the offshore regions of Indonesia. Should North African and other Middle East nations succeed in establishing an effective petroleum "conference," it would influence but still not dominate the situation.

More immediately relevant is the current shift in the position of the USSR from an oil exporter to an oil importer, accounting for its loans and assistance to Syria, Iraq, and Egypt for oil drilling and explorations. The question arises as to whether these countries would fare better under Soviet auspices than they have with the private oil companies of the West. What will be the ratio of oil royalties to total value when these countries face the Soviet Union instead of a single oil company? Will it continue to be said, as it has been in Iraq and elsewhere, that the oil operations have set the pace for wages in the whole economy? Will the transportation of oil to the users' markets be easier or more difficult? How will payment be made? Or are these eventualities so remote as not to condition the oil prosperity of the Middle East?

Foreign Capital

Two countries included in the present study have experienced a *deus ex machina* for economic development from an inflow of foreign grant or loan capital instead of petroleum royalties. In the case of Turkey, most of the funds have been American economic and military aid, aggregating $5 billion to 1968, aside from considerably smaller sums from other members of the Consortium since 1963 and from foreign private capital. In the case of Egypt, it was the liquidation of the sterling balances accumulated during the second world war (amounting to E£ 440 million, or the equivalent of ten years' imports at the 1945 rate) that financed the balance-of-payments deficit initially. Later the burden was carried by American aid, amounting to $900 million by 1968, Russian loans, and the contributions made by Arab oil-producing countries, substituting for the missing Suez revenues.

Whatever its origin, foreign aid played an important role in the development of both countries, especially during the fifties to the economic downturn of 1957–58. American tractors supplied the sinews of the large increase of agricultural output in Turkey in those years. Public Law 480 wheat helped to feed the populace of Egypt; later Soviet finance and technicians built the Aswan Dam. In the case of neither country could the amounts of foreign aid compare with the oil revenues accruing to some other countries. But it is generally agreed that foreign capital provided marginal but probably essential assistance to the development of Turkey and Egypt.

The appraisal of American aid in the Middle East, both from the government and from private eleemosynary sources, should not be limited to a strictly economic accounting, including its important contributions to technical knowledge and productive skills. The cultural impact has been very great also. Indeed, seasoned travelers in the region report a large amount of goodwill toward the United States, existing even in some countries which have broken off diplomatic relations.

To return to the dollars and cents side of the matter, inflows of foreign grants and loans are not only smaller than outflows of oil, but are also more temporary. They are, indeed, self-limiting, for either the creditors' and donors' patience is exhausted or the service of the debt exceeds the flow of new credits. Turkey's creditors banded together in a Consortium to fund the debt and stretch out the amortization, but with the understanding that new lending would not be considered except for extreme emergency. Egypt's foreign trade deficit can be improved only by denying improvements in the standard of living of a people who have long expected that some of the promised fruits from casting out the foreigners and from the nationalizations would materialize. Thus, from Middle East experience, as well as elsewhere, supplies of foreign capital, regarded at the time of Truman's Point Four as the fulcrum of development, now prove to be merely auxiliary at the beginning but not a sustaining vital factor. And the termination of the capital inflow is a painful process.

Labor Force

Unemployment in some guise or other is a very nearly universal mark of the less-developed countries, and the five countries which have been reviewed are no exception. In Egypt and elsewhere the unemployed on the land drift into the cities, augmenting the slums and the excessive number of persons engaged in domestic service, where, at least, they do no harm. Government service absorbs and conceals much of the potential unemployment in more sophisticated circles, including the younger generation coming from the universities. This does much harm: increasing bureaucratic red tape, burdening the budget, producing inflation, and demoralizing the populace. "Unlimited supply of labor," once viewed as a potential source of development even for the poorest of countries, may instead make them poorer.

One remedy for unemployment is illustrated by Lebanon, which, like Ireland, has for generations supplied the world with energetic and enterprising emigrants. Beside reducing domestic unemployment, this perennial exodus has resulted in a return flow of emigrants' remittances, and—upon the return of these people to their native land—a supply of progressive business and technological ideas. For Turkey there is another sort of safety valve in the seasonal movement of Turkish laborers to work in Western Europe. In recent years this item in the balance of payments has not been inconsiderable, amounting sometimes to as much as one-fifth the value of visible exports. Again, a certain amount of mechanical knowledge and a certain infiltration of modern and democratic ideas accrue to the country upon the return of seasonal laborers to their homes.

Such adjustments, however, are mere palliatives of rural and urban unemployment in the Middle East. Fundamentally and in the long run, the remedies are two: education, especially trade and technical training, and—even more basic and necessary—reduction of population growth. These two topics are considered briefly later.

Iran has employed an ingenious device which "kills several birds with one stone"—the establishment of the Health Corps, Knowledge Corps, and Productivity Corps. By converting unskilled to skilled labor, they reduce unemployment among the unskilled, where it is most severe. All three of the corps raise productivity and national income. Finally by utilizing the energies of the young recruits in productive activity, they raise the quality and morale of the military establishment.

Economic Systems

One motive for choosing exactly the five countries of this study was to observe the difference in performance of collectivist compared to individualist systems. The results, it must be confessed, are less than completely satisfactory. For example, while

Egypt parades under the banner of socialism and Turkey's system is referred to as capitalism, the difference between the two regimes is not categoric. In both countries, the greater part of industry, including all large and important undertakings, is government controlled. State ownership or control extends in both to banking and finance of all categories. What remains for private ownership and enterprise is agriculture and small-scale trading. These characteristics apply in about the same degree to Iraq.

Even the chief shortcomings of their systems are very similar in Turkey and Egypt.[1] Both have operated with large and worrisome deficits in the balance of payments; both have allowed unrealistic rates of exchange to persist, Turkey more conspicuously than Egypt; both suffer from artificial and unrealistic prices, i.e., inconsistent and unsystematic interrelations; and both are burdened with a clumsy and excessive bureaucracy, though in this case it is Egypt which suffers to a greater degree.

Nevertheless, the differences between Turkish etatism and Arab socialism, which have been set forth at an earlier juncture, are real. But a review of their nature reveals that they are less matters of mechanical working of the economic systems than of attitudes, intentions, and politics. The orientation of Turkey is western, democratic, parliamentary, and liberal; that of Egypt is eastern, Arabic, and authoritarian. So stated, these contrasts are too categoric and there are domestic strains between the two tendencies. But the differing general tone is unmistakable.

The one really contrasting economic system is Lebanon's which is genuinely free enterprise despite an expanded role of state investment in recent years. A brief reference to pages dealing with this country will recall that it has registered an impressive number of "firsts," including various economic rates in increase, high GNP per capita and highest levels in important welfare matters. The relative freedom from distortions within the economic system characterizing other countries of the Middle East, as well as the absence of a burdensome bureaucracy, are strikingly evident. Lebanon can well be an object of emulation in many ways. But one must recognize that its history and the very fabric of its society and economy are unique. Its position in the Middle East as a commercial and financial center almost automatically places it in the free private enterprise category. No other nation in the region, including even Israel, promises to rival it in these functions, at least as long as Lebanon does not disintegrate under the impact of hostile neighbors or their agents within the country. Probably also, other countries in the region cannot, as a matter of *Realpolitik*, very soon or very extensively transform themselves into Lebanon's liberal regime, even if they so desired.

Iran is not as clearly characterized as a private enterprise economy as Lebanon. It is nevertheless strongly imbued with that philosophy, despite the many fields permeated by government controls or operations. Iran belongs with the numerous "mixed" economies, in leaving agriculture to the farmers, but with fewer interventions by the state than in Egypt, for example. Many financial and industrial undertakings are private; government credit and import tariffs are definitely oriented toward fostering individual enterprise. These, and some of the welfare measures, strengthen the middle class and hence contribute to political stability and economic growth.

Around the middle of the past decade, it looked as if the processes of nationalization and the growth of socialism in Egypt, Iraq, and Syria had reached a limit. In Iraq, the government of Premier Bazzaz liquidated the office which had been created

---

[1] Iraq is a case apart, inasmuch as its principal difficulties are political rather than economic.

111

to run nationalized enterprises; it declared that both the private and public sectors are important. In Egypt, a National Production Conference issued a manifesto welcoming private enterprise. Even Syria denationalized some smaller industrial concerns. But the six-day war interrupted or ended this process; meantime the course of intense nationalism and nationalization has held sway, and the future holds no promise for definable change.

Economic Institutions

The Distribution of Wealth and Income

The Middle East shares the characteristic of nearly all of the less-developed world that income and wealth are highly unequal, much more so than in Western Europe, North America, and other countries classed as "developed." Generally speaking also, the wealthy are so few in number that an equal sharing of wealth and income would do little to improve the lot of the poor. Thus the redistribution of land, which has gone farther in Egypt than anywhere else, has not much increased the income of the fellahin. In Turkey, land reform in the sense of redistribution has not been actively prosecuted for this reason. In Iraq, land reform has been a halting process.

In Iran, the wealthy landowning class has been "bought out" with government oil revenues, and the state has sponsored liberal mortgage policies for the new small land holders. Agricultural productivity has been furthered by central government policies, which have also played a frankly egalitarian role through cheap mortgage credit. The contributions of United States AID to agriculture have supported expansion in rural education, improvement in commodity marketing, and the fostering of mechanization.

In the West, extreme inequality has yielded to measures along two principal routes—progressive taxation and direct welfare measures which benefit the poor more than the rich. Progressive taxation cannot be a powerful instrument unless the tax system itself is rationally planned and effectively enforced. The Middle East, aside from Israel, has not in general achieved either, especially as income taxation—the classical vehicle for progressive rates—is hard to apply to agriculture, which includes large fractions of the population, and impossible to enforce where financial records are lacking, a usual result of widespread illiteracy.

Where there is a prosperous and highly literate middle class, income taxation would be successful if tax morality matched the other prerequisites. Unfortunately, in Lebanon, the only country of the present study enjoying the first set of prerequisites, this type of morality seems to be lacking with the business and professional classes—the latter to greater degree than the former—evasion approaching 90 percent! In conditions prevailing there and generally in the Middle East, the fiscal avenue toward lessening inequality has not thus far been successful.

Turning then to welfare, especially in its equalitarian aspects, we find that since the end of the first world war the great inequality between the sexes in the Muslim world has been more markedly diminished than economic inequality in general. Beginning with the Ataturk revolution in Turkey, this change has spread through most of the Middle East. Lebanon, being until recently more than half Christian, had the smallest distance to traverse. In Egypt and Iran, virtual freedom of entry to all business, professional, and government careers obtains for women. In somewhat lesser degree this holds true elsewhere, although in some countries, and in the rural areas generally, women have not yet escaped from an inferior status. Statistics of enrollment in the schools and universities show a large increase, both proportionally and absolutely, of women students.

Welfare has undoubtedly been somewhat increased by the general increase in school and university enrollments, though this would be impossible to assess quantitatively. So too with land reform. In Egypt, where redistribution of land has been coupled with the growth of cooperatives and the spread of rural community centers, the welfare of the peasants has risen with improved health, literacy, and tenancy conditions despite the failure of per capita wages to rise. Elsewhere land reform has, in general, been attended with certain nonpecuniary benefits.

The welfare of labor in most countries may have risen where per capita income for the whole society has increased, but because of the increase of populations, the increase has generally been small or negligible, except in Iran. Labor unions, with the exception of Lebanon among the countries studied, have been weak and unable to bargain effectively for higher wages, the power to strike either having been only recently acquired or being "temporarily" held in abeyance.

Welfare generally defies quantitative measurement. But it appears to be plausible on balance that welfare gains for the mass of population in the Middle East have been very modest, or in some countries nonexistent, despite record increases in aggregate gross national product. Partly this is explained by military expenditures, partly by a failure of newly acquired wealth to "trickle down" to the common man, but mostly by the high rates of population increase.

Economic Planning

Turkey inaugurated its first economic plan, perhaps the first in the world outside of the USSR, in 1933. Despite its designation as a Five Year Plan and its undoubted inspiration from the East, the plan was a far cry from the global centralized planning of the Soviet Union. Economic activity came gradually to be dominated by the government but only halfway under its direct control. Even in the more inclusive Five Year Plans of 1963–67 and 1967–72, Turkey remains a mixed economy. The years of most rapid growth came in 1950–58 under the influence of good crops, rapid agricultural expansion, and the Korean boom, not as a consequence of planning.

Lebanon, as befits a predominantly free enterprise country, was one of the last countries in the Middle East to institute planning, in 1963. The prosperity of the nation grew fairly consistently after the second world war with setbacks in 1957 and 1958 and limited growth quite recently. The Development Plan set afoot in the mid-sixties pertains mostly to the retarded but less important field of agriculture.

In Egypt, the political revolution of 1952 preceded by eight years the fairly thoroughgoing first Five Year Plan of 1960–65 and by nine years the wave of nationalizations of 1961–63. The chief land reform measure came immediately after the revolution and the Helwan steel plant was begun shortly thereafter. Egypt scored its largest growth rates before the Suez war of 1956.

Shortly after the beginning of the great increase of its petroleum production, Iraq established its Development Board and allocated 30 percent of the revenues to this purpose. In this country, development planning occupied a central position from

1950 to the Revolution of 1958. The size of the oil royalties produced large increases in the gross national product both before, during, and after the period of intense planning.

Partly because of the early economic missions to Iran—Millspaugh (1922–27) and Morrison Knudsen (1947)—government oil revenues came to be largely devoted to economic development. But the first Plan (1948–55) was anything but comprehensive; the second Plan (1955–62) was detoured for the largest government projects; only with the third Plan (1962–68) did planning become fairly comprehensive. How much investment within the planning framework is public and how much is private varies considerably with different cabinets and the changing convictions of the Shah.

Individual chapters devoted to each of these countries have pointed to the strong and weak points of planning in each case. On the whole, the Plans probably contributed to growth, but planning sometimes preceded rapid growth, sometimes followed it, and sometimes seemed to have little relation to it. Planning can be associated with free enterprise, and it is not necessarily a part of socialism. In the Middle East, planning is still in an experimental and sometimes amorphous state.

Education, Religion, Individual Behavior

All of the countries of this study report large increases in the number of students at all levels of the educational process and substantial gains in the percentage of literacy. Lest these figures convey too favorable an impression, it is well to remember several facts. In the first place, despite these increases, the educational level of the masses—with the exception of Lebanon—is still relatively low. Iraq, for example, was obliged to report that only one-fourth to one-third of the school age population (5–19 years) could actually attend. Also the prevalent high drop-out rates spell a virtual waste of the schooling secured in the beginning years. A widespread criticism of the educational systems of most of the Middle East countries is that they do little or nothing to prepare the scholars or students for economically useful roles. Indeed, in some cases the end result may even be negative, because the excessively cultural preoccupation of the curricula may instill in the students a disdainful attitude toward hard work. The situation in the University of Cairo is open not only to this objection but also to the further wastage involved in admitting all comers, regardless of their quality as students. Compounding the loss is the rule that university graduates, again without regard to qualifications, are given government jobs if they so choose. The founding of technical schools and colleges in Turkey, Iran, and Iraq is a step in the right direction, but the process could be carried much further.

Religion in the Middle East has both its good and its negative aspects from the angle of economic development. In times past it was believed that the Islamic faith implanted an aloofness from economic motivation. Both attitudes, where present, impede economic effort, efficiency, and development. There was also a traditional preference among young men for careers in government, the army, and the professions rather than business, finance, manufacturing, and the mechanical arts. Since the end of the first world war, these religious and social attitudes appear to have waned. They no longer constitute serious obstacles to national economic growth. But where, as in the Middle East, religion or culture, such as Arabism or Judaism, takes on a frenetic intensity, it can breed political incompatibility and armed conflict.

The Demographic Problem

The historical association of large and increasing populations with national glory or well-being has been definitively broken by sheer technological and economic facts. Military power no longer depends upon masses of troops. Economic productivity no longer depends upon large supplies of labor, at least of the undifferentiated sorts. Indeed, high rates of population increase are more apt to frustrate than to enhance the potential military power of a nation and its rate of economic development.

Political Stability

One of the most dramatic demonstrations which comes from the comparison of the five countries of the present study is the cost of domestic instability and the gains of stable government. That Turkey, not especially favored in other ways, could attain satisfactory rates of economic growth is attributable in considerable measure to stable government. The story of Iraq's development bears eloquent witness to the contrast between periods of relative calm and of turbulence. Iran's phenomenal development has come during the decade and a half since the last political upheaval in 1951–53.

American Policy

The present study has not been oriented toward recommendations concerning United States economic—or still less, political—policy in the Middle East. Nevertheless, it would be pointless to refrain from drawing some inference on policy from the several chapters and some further observations consonant with their positions.

With regard to the merits of private enterprise and of socialism in the economic development of Middle Eastern countries, the American government has in general, as indeed seems to be appropriate, maintained a position of noninterference, aside from obvious indirect influences. Business and producer firms of the United States can be counted upon to give lively demonstrations of the efficacy of private enterprise, at least when they are permitted by the national government to operate at all. Nowhere is this more in evidence than in Iran, where U.S. companies have invested $150 million, aside from oil installations, in the past five years. Some hundred firms of American origin have made their contribution to the present 10.5 percent annual increase of GNP. It scarcely needs argument that the American government should encourage these activities in all ways short of subsidy.

At the same time, the United States government recognizes that private enterprise alone cannot fulfill all the needs of less developed countries. The United States practiced noninterference in domestic politics, for example, by continuing economic aid to Egypt for a decade after Nasser declared his intention of making Egypt a socialist country; and American economic aid to the avowed private enterprise economy of Lebanon never amounted to enough to account for that country's prosperity. Political and military considerations undoubtedly play a certain role; but it has rarely been charged that United States aid was utilized as an instrument to promote "capitalism" within the recipient countries. Indeed, partly through no fault of its own, international capitalism has not recently been a potent political factor in the Middle East. There have been no activist free-enterprise domestic parties paralleling the international Communist parties, which have been barred in most of the region. The West in general, and the United States in particular, vociferously charged with imperialism and other sins, has not been taxed with this sort of subversion.

What are the major concerns of United States policy in the Middle East? The answer may well run in terms of four objectives,[2] of which one is political, one partly economic and partly political, and two are primarily economic. The political objective, prevention of aggression by any country in the Middle East area, may be outside the concern of this essay. American policy has come a long way since the enunciation in 1947 of the Truman Doctrine of keeping the USSR out of the Middle East, however necessary the pronouncement was at the time. But United States military and economic aid in substantial volume to such peripheral nations as Greece, Turkey, and Iran (to say nothing of Iraq and Pakistan) has undoubtedly deterred possible Soviet aggression in these nations. American "intervention," if such it may be called, was welcomed by the governments involved, and there seem to be no adequate grounds for regrets or for repudiating the bilateral defense alliances stemming from 1959 or earlier. To do so would degrade the United States not only in the eyes of these friendly nations, but in the eyes of less friendly countries as well.

Since the Soviet Union has chosen the Arab countries, and not Israel, as the repository of its ambitions in the Middle East, the issue of Soviet power is inextricably intermingled with the Israeli-Arab conflict. The past history of United States policy in this matter is subject to divergent interpretations, particularly since United States aid to Egypt was relatively generous (in comparison to other Middle East countries) both before the Czech offer of arms and during the period 1960–63. However, after the suspension of possible financial and technical aid on the Aswan project, American aid dwindled to the vanishing point by 1967, confirming Arab suspicions of an American bias favorable to Israel. The only possible answer to these suspicions would be a reaffirmation of American political neutrality, which would also be a reaffirmation of the Eisenhower policy against aggression in *any* quarter. In practical affairs, this seems to involve the balancing off of military power in the Israeli-Arab conflict; but the means of achieving this objective lie outside the sphere of economic policy.

The limitation of Soviet influence in the Middle East, on the other hand, is partly an economic matter. Here again, American efforts will eventually have to stand upon the record. While the United States undoubtedly lost a great deal of prestige over the Aswan episode, its sober advice as to the use of foreign and domestic funds for development must have won respect over the years. Much of the American effort, in Turkey, Iraq, and Iran has gone into the advancement of agriculture, public health, and education. These less glamorous efforts at investment would seem to indicate the intent of the donor to benefit the recipient country, not merely to purchase allegiance by showcase projects. Furthermore, by such measures the incomes and welfare of the poorer and lower middle-class strata have been improved, lessening the impulses toward such political extremism as communism. In the long run, American and West European business enterprise in the Middle East, conjoined with aid by governments and international agencies, should demonstrate the fact that development aspirations and development plans can be realized under democratic auspices.

---

[2] A useful analysis is presented in The American Assembly, Georgiana G. Stevens, ed., *The United States and the Middle East* (Englewood Cliffs, N.J.: Prentice-Hall, Inc., 1964), p. 177, *et seq.*

Aside from illustrating the viability of an economy based on personal freedom and price-system governance, American objectives in the Middle East embrace two economic aims which are more specific: the continued flow of oil to Western markets, and American access to the commodity and capital markets of the region. United States trade and investment in this area, including North Africa, yield an inflow of income into this country of $2 billion annually, chiefly from petroleum. American concern with the supply of oil is indirect, since only a small fraction enters the United States market. But any interruption of the supply going to the major market, which is West European, would entail a switch to American sources and produce at least temporary shortages on both sides of the Atlantic. Secondly, the flow of oil is, of course, vital to the oil companies' survival. By the same token, however, Middle East countries have a large stake in the continued flow of oil to Europe. While the threat of nationalization is ever present, amounting in some cases to a practical certainty in the long run, the dependence of the oil-producing countries on the European market and upon foreign transportation and marketing facilities bids fair to put a limit on the exaction of higher royalties. Thus American firms may survive and even flourish despite nationalizations.

The United States also has an interest in maintaining its exports to and its commodity imports from the Middle East. In this matter, however, it enjoys a twofold advantage. For one thing, it has the considerable protection of being either an important seller or an important buyer of some principal export or import with virtually every country studied. But, because of the size of American national income and its international trade, the fraction of total exports or imports involved with the Middle East is not great. Thus, the United States participation possesses a strategic advantage. In the second place, in many of its export lines the United States enjoys a significant buyers' preference. In the long run, this advantage—shared with some European and Japanese producers—could be expected to erode the system of bilateral trading agreements which recently has bound Egypt and other socialist countries to the USSR and its satellites.

The tenor of the foregoing observations on desirable United States policies for dealing with the Middle East rests upon an optimistic view of the intrinsic value and the ultimate appeal of American motives in its foreign relations. It also rests upon an optimistic view of the competitiveness of American productive techniques, exportable know-how, and business methods. This being the case, a similar philosophy of reasonable self-confidence should underlie United States foreign aid. It need not always be conditioned upon an anti-Soviet stance on the part of the recipient, though countries friendly to the United States are likely to be accorded more generous treatment.

Useful deductions regarding economic development which can be derived from the preceding five country studies are applicable roughly proportionally to the internal political stability of the country and its peaceful international relations. But American economic aid need not await complete pacification in the Middle East; indeed, economic aid might contribute something toward that end.

Aid for economically feasible projects, not necessarily on a grandiose scale, could be offered to Arab and non-Arab countries alike, whether they profess to call themselves friend or foe. The granting of aid to nations professedly hostile to the United States would be a conciliatory gesture; it could lead to a slowly improving relationship. At the least, the sojourn of aid personnel would add to the "presence" of the United States, already represented *entre autres* by the USIA libraries, the Peace Corps, the Robert College in Istanbul, and American Universities at Beirut and Cairo, at a time when the honeymoon period of some Middle East countries with the USSR may become less romantic than erstwhile. Misgivings concerning strengthening the economy of an unfriendly state by economic aid can largely be put aside, inasmuch as modern weaponry does not depend as directly on the strength of the economy as did the older conventional armaments. By directing aid toward public health and education, particularly trades schools and technical high schools, American aid could help to alleviate a very deficient part of Middle East manpower, with popular equalitarian appeal in the bargain. Meanwhile, in some instances, military aid could be shifted toward the economic, and the United States could channel more aid into international agencies.

There never has been any reality in the idea of the United States as an imperialist country. American foreign policy and American economic relations must be managed in the Middle East so as to display this fact conspicuously. Furthermore the United States government must even "lean over backward" in its policy of even-handed treatment of Israel and the Arab states, because of the "unofficial favoritism" toward Israel which arises from the large sums which have flowed into that country from American private donors.

APPENDIX

U.S. LOANS AND GRANTS 1946–68: MIDDLE EAST
Total less repayments and interest, U.S. fiscal years
(in millions of dollars)

	Economic			Military
	Total	Loans	Grants	
Cyprus	20.3	1.2	19.0	—
Greece	1,672.1	113.5	1,558.7	1,952.0
Iran	769.6	317.1	452.7	1,153.5
Iraq	49.9	20.6	29.3	46.7
Israel	784.7	415.7	369.0	16.7 [a]
Jordan	575.0	19.0	556.0	65.9 [a]
Kuwait	49.4	49.4	—	—
Lebanon	74.7	2.6	72.1	8.9
Saudi Arabia	36.3	8.8	27.5	n.a.
Syria	60.0	20.9	39.0	0.1
Turkey	2,231.3	1,083.0	1,148.2	2,963.6
UAR	900.9	607.9	293.0	—
Yemen	42.7	—	42.7	—
Totals	7,266.9	2,659.7	4,607.2	6,207.4

[a] Through 1967.
Source: Compiled from U.S. AID *Economic Data Book: Near East and South Asia.*

SOURCES

I. Books

Adams, Doris G. *Iraq's People and Resources*. Berkeley: University of California Press, 1958.

American Assembly, Georgiana G. Stevens, editor. *The United States and the Middle East*. Englewood Cliffs, N.J.: Prentice-Hall, 1964.

Aryamehr, Mohammed Reza Pahlavi. *The White Revolution*. Teheran: The Imperial Library, 2d ed., 1967.

Baldwin, George B. *Planning and Development in Iran*. Baltimore: Johns Hopkins Press, 1967.

Berger, Morroe. *The Arab World Today*. Garden City, N.Y.: Doubleday & Co., Inc., 1964.

Commission on International Development. *Partners in Development*. New York: Praeger Publishers, 1969.

Farahmand, Sohrab. *Der Wirtschaftsaufbau des Iran*. Basel: Kyklos, 1965.

Grunwald, Kurt, and Ronall, Joachim O. *Industrialization in the Middle East*. New York: Council for Middle East Affairs Press, 1950.

Hansen, B., and Marzouk, G. *Development and Economic Policy in the UAR (Egypt)*. Amsterdam: North Holland Publishing Co., 1965.

Herschlag, Z. Y. *Turkey: The Challenge of Growth*. Leiden, Netherlands: E. J. Brill, 1968.

———. *Turkey: An Economy in Transition*. The Hague: van Keulen, n.d., preface, 1958.

Hitti, Philip K. *Lebanon in History*. London: Macmillan Co., 3rd ed., 1967.

Institut de Formation en vue du Développement. *Le Liban Face à son Développement*. Begrouth, 1963.

Iranian-American Economic Survey 1967. New York: Manhattan Publishing Co., n.d.

Issawi, Charles. *Egypt in Revolution, An Economic Analysis*. London: Oxford University Press, 1963.

Jacobs, Norman. *The Sociology of Development: Iran as an Asian Case Study*. New York: Frederick A. Praeger, Inc., 1966.

Kermani, Taghi T. *Economic Development in Action: Theories, Problems, and Procedures as Applied in the Middle East*. Cleveland, Ohio: The World Publishing Company, 1967.

Langley, Kathleen M. *The Industrialization of Iraq*. Cambridge: Harvard University Press, 1961.

Lenczowski, George. *The Middle East in World Affairs*. Ithaca, N.Y.: Cornell University Press, 3d ed., 1962.

Lewis, Bernard. *The Middle East and West*. Bloomington, Ind.: Indiana University Press, 1964.

Mead, Donald C. *Growth and Structural Change in the Egyptian Economy*. Homewood, Ill.: Richard D. Irwin, Inc., 1967.

Meyer, A. J. *Middle Eastern Capitalism*. Cambridge, Mass.: Harvard University Press, 1959.

121

O'Brien, Patrick. *The Revolution in Egypt's Economic System: From Private Enterprise to Socialism 1952–1965*. Royal Institute of International Affairs. London: Oxford University Press, 1966.

Peretz, Don. *The Middle East Today*. New York: Holt, Rinehart and Winston, Inc., 1963.

Qubain, F. I. *The Reconstruction of Iraq 1950–1957*. New York: Frederick A. Praeger, Inc., 1958.

Robinson, Richard D. *The First Turkish Republic, A Case Study in National Development*. Cambridge, Mass.: Harvard University Press, 1965.

————. *High-Level Manpower in Economic Development: The Turkish Case*. Cambridge: Harvard University Press, 1967.

Royal Institute of International Affairs, Sir Reader Bullard, editor. *The Middle East: A Political and Economic Survey*, 3d ed., London: Oxford University Press, 1958.

Sayigh, Yusif A. *Entrepreneurs of Lebanon*. Cambridge: Harvard University Press, 1963.

Thompson, J. H., and Reischauer, R. D., editors. *Modernization of the Arab World*. Princeton, N.J.: D. Van Nostrand Co., Inc., 1966.

Thornburg, M. W.; Spry, Graham; and Soule, George. *Turkey: An Economic Appraisal*. New York: The Twentieth-Century Fund, 1949.

Warriner, Doreen. *Land Reform and Development in the Middle East, A Study of Egypt, Syria, and Iraq*, 2d ed., London: Oxford University Press, 1962.

Wilber, Donald N. *Iran, Past and Present*. Princeton, N.J.: Princeton University Press, 5th ed., 1963.

II. Journal Articles and Contributions to Symposia

Amuzegar, Jahangir. "Nationalism vs. Economic Growth." *Foreign Affairs*, July 1966, pp. 650–61.

Chase Manhattan Bank, New York. "Lebanon, Special Country Report," *World Business*, July 1968.

Hansen, Bent. "Planning and Economic Growth in Egypt, 1960–1965," *Egypt Since the Revolution*. Edited by P. J. Vatikiotis. London: Allen and Unwin, 1968.

Issawi, Charles. "Economic Development and Liberalism in Lebanon." *The Middle East Journal*, Summer 1964, pp. 279–92. Also in *Politics in Lebanon*. Edited by Leonard Binder. New York: John Wiley & Sons, Inc., 1966.

Karpat, Kemal H. "Socialism and the Labor Party of Turkey." *The Middle East Journal*, Spring 1967, pp. 157–72.

Khuri, Fuad I. "The Changing Class Structure in Lebanon." *The Middle East Journal*, Winter 1969, pp. 29–44.

Langley, Kathleen M. "Iraq: Some Aspects of the Economic Scene." *The Middle East Journal*, Spring 1964, pp. 180–88.

Lenczowski, George. "Iraq: Seven Years of Revolution." *Current History*, May 1965, pp. 281–89. Reprinted as No. 182, Middle Eastern Series, Institute of International Studies, University of California, Berkeley.

————. "Oil in the Middle East." *Current History*, May 1960, pp. 262–67.

Okyar, Osman. "Inflation in a Mixed Economy." *Capital Formation and Investment in Industry*, pp. 352–70. Istanbul: Economic and Social Studies Conference Board, 1963.

Peretz, Don. "River Schemes and the Effect on Economic Development in Jordan, Syria, and Lebanon." *The Middle East Journal*, Summer 1964, pp. 293–305.

Salem, Elie. "Cabinet Politics in Lebanon." *The Middle East Journal*, Autumn 1967, pp. 488–502.

Watts, D. C. "Second Thoughts About the Military." *The New Middle East*, September 1969, pp. 36–37.

Yasa, Memduh. "Marshalling of Capital by the State and Direct Investment in Industry: Turkish Experience." *Capital Formation and Investment in Industry*, pp. 94–99. Istanbul: Economic and Social Studies Conference Board, 1963.

III. Journals, Newspapers, and Government Publications

Agency for International Development. AID *Economic Data Book: Near East and South Asia*. Washington, D. C., December 1968, and later supplements.

———. Office of Program and Policy Development, Statistics and Reports Division. *Gross National Product: Growth Rates and Trend Data by Region and Country*. Washington, D.C., April 25, 1969.

———. *U.S. Foreign Aid in the Near East and South Asia*. Washington, D.C., n.d.

Economist Intelligence Unit (London). *Iran: Quarterly Economic Reviews. Iran: Annual Supplements*.

Egypt, National Bank of. *Economic Bulletin*.

International Monetary Fund. *Balance of Payments Yearbook*.

———. *International Financial Statistics*.

Iran, Central Bank of. *Annual Reports*.

Iran, Bank Melli. *30 Years of Bank Melli Iran, 1928–1958*.

Iran News and Documents, Ministry of Information, Teheran, Iran, Vol. I, No. 50, March 9, 1970.

Iraq, Central Bank of. *Annual Reports*.

Iraq, Republic of. Ministry of Planning, Central Statistical Organization. *Quarterly Bulletin of Statistics*.

The Los Angeles Times.

Middle East Business Digest.

The Middle East Journal.

The New Middle East.

Turkey, Republic of. State Planning Organization. *First Five-Year Development Plan, 1963-1967*. Ankara: Central Bank of the Republic of Turkey, 1964.

———. *Second Five-Year Development Plan, 1968–1972*. Ankara: Central Bank of the Republic of Turkey, 1969.

Turkish Economic Review.

United Arab Republic. *Statistical Handbook*.

United Nations. *Economic Developments in the Middle East*.

———. *World Economic Survey*.

Legislative and Special Analyses Published to Date, 91st Congress, Second Session:

LEGISLATIVE HISTORY, 91st CONGRESS, 1st SESSION, AND INDEX OF AEI PUBLICATIONS

OVERVIEW OF THE FISCAL 1971 FEDERAL BUDGET

THE VETERANS HOME LOAN FINANCING BILL

THE BILL TO REVAMP THE WELFARE SYSTEM

U.S. GOVERNMENT FINANCES: A 22-YEAR PERSPECTIVE, 1950-1971 ($3.00 per copy)

PROPOSALS TO CONTROL THE COST OF DRUGS UNDER FEDERAL HEALTH AND WELFARE PROGRAMS

POSTAL REFORM PROPOSALS

FOREIGN TRADE BILLS

REVENUE SHARING BILLS

HOW CAN OUR PHYSICAL ENVIRONMENT BEST BE CONTROLLED AND DEVELOPED? (High School Debate Topic)

THE ABM SAFEGUARD SYSTEM (Rev. Ed.) ($3.00)

WHAT PACE WITHDRAWAL? THE McGOVERN-HATFIELD AMENDMENT

THE CRIME CONTROL AND SAFE STREETS BILL

THE PROPOSAL TO ACCELERATE PAYMENT OF ESTATE AND GIFT TAXES

POLITICAL ACTIVITIES OF COLLEGES AND UNIVERSITIES: SOME POLICY AND LEGAL IMPLICATIONS ($3.00)

THE PENDING SOCIAL SECURITY AMENDMENTS OF 1970

MANPOWER DEVELOPMENT AND TRAINING PROPOSALS

TRENDS IN PRESCRIPTION DRUG PRICES ($3.00)

PRIVATE ENTERPRISE AND SOCIALISM IN THE MIDDLE EAST ($3.00 per copy)

THE DILEMMA OF ISRAEL ($3.00 per copy)

TRADE PATTERNS IN THE MIDDLE EAST ($3.00 per copy)

Recent Long-Range Studies

Mikesell, Raymond F. THE U.S. BALANCE OF PAYMENTS AND THE INTERNATIONAL ROLE OF THE DOLLAR. July 1970.

Peterson, John M. and Stewart, Charles T., Jr. EMPLOYMENT EFFECTS OF MINIMUM WAGE RATES. August 1969.

Goetz, Raymond. TAX TREATMENT OF PENSION PLANS—Preferential or Normal? April 1969.

Haberler, Gottfried and Willett, Thomas D. U.S. BALANCE OF PAYMENTS POLICIES AND INTERNATIONAL MONETARY REFORM: A CRITICAL ANALYSIS. September 1968.

Huston, Luther A.; Miller, Arthur Selwyn; Krislov, Samuel; and Dixon, Robert G., Jr. ROLES OF THE ATTORNEY GENERAL OF THE UNITED STATES. July 1968.

Middle East Series

UNITED STATES INTERESTS IN THE MIDDLE EAST ($3.00 per copy)

DOCUMENTS ON THE MIDDLE EAST ($3.00 per copy)

JERUSALEM: KEYSTONE OF AN ARAB-ISRAELI SETTLEMENT

PRIVATE ENTERPRISE AND SOCIALISM IN THE MIDDLE EAST ($3.00 per copy)

THE DILEMMA OF ISRAEL ($3.00 per copy)

TRADE PATTERNS IN THE MIDDLE EAST ($3.00 per copy)

Antitrust Compendium

ANTITRUST CONSENT DECREES, 1906-1966—Compendium of Abstracts ($30.00 per copy)

1967-1968 SUPPLEMENT TO ANTITRUST CONSENT DECREES ($10.00 per copy)

Analyses and Studies: $2.00 per copy except as indicated
Discounts: 25 to 99 copies—20%; 100 to 299 copies—30%;
300 to 499 copies—40%; 500 and over—50%.

AMERICAN ENTERPRISE INSTITUTE
1200 17th Street, N.W., Washington, D.C. 20036